○ WRITING **HISTORIES**

IMAGINATION AND NARRATION

WRITING **HISTORIES**

IMAGINATION AND NARRATION

EDITED BY **ANN CURTHOYS** AND **ANN MCGRATH**

MONASH University
ePress

Updated edition published in 2009 by
Monash University ePress
Building 4, Monash University
Clayton, Victoria, 3800, Australia
www.epress.monash.edu.au

DESIGN
AKDesign (www.akdesign.com.au)

COVER IMAGE
© Mandy Martin and Tom Griffiths. Detail from *Flood below the Shearing Shed. 16 February*. 1999. Oil, ochre, pigment on linen. 90x330 cms. The painting is from the environmental project: Watersheds; the Paroo to the Warrego 1999. www.mandy-martin.com

PRINTER
Sydney University Publishing Service

This book is available online at www.epress.monash.edu/wh

ISBN: 978-0-9804648-2-5 (pb)
ISBN: 978-0-9804648-3-2 (web)

First published in 2000 by
Monash Publications in History
School of Historical Studies
Monash University
Clayton, Victoria, 3800, Australia

Pages: 124

CONTENTS

A note about pagination and chapter identification

Page numbers in this book do not run consecutively across chapters. Instead, page numbering restarts on the first page of each chapter and is prefaced by the chapter number. Thus 01.1 is chapter 1, page 1; 01.2 is chapter 1, page 2; 02.1 is chapter 2, page 1; 02.2 is chapter 2, page 2; and so on.

In the Table of Contents, each chapter is listed with its chapter number (01, 02, 03, etc.) only.

This system, in which page numbering is self-contained within each chapter, allows the publisher, Monash University ePress, to publish individual chapters online.

ACKNOWLEDGEMENTS

We have many people to thank. Those who helped this book come about include, first, our contributors, who have been a pleasure to work with and who gave freely of their time to the Visiting Scholars Program at the Centre for Cross-Cultural Research at the Australian National University in April 1999.

We also thank the students in that program for their enthusiasm, commitment and thoughtful feedback. They were: Michael Adams, Bernie Brian, Alison Cadzow, Sumedha Dhani, Ruth Lane, Chris Lefler, Damian Lucas, Kirsten Mackay, Sue Hardisty, Minoru Hokari, Jill Rundle, Ann Standish, Bill Wilson and Charles Zuber. We also wish to thank Michael Adams, Bernie Brian, Sue Hardisty, Ann Standish and Bill Wilson for permission to quote them. Thanks are also due to the students we have separately taught in other 'Writing History' classes, at the Australian National University, the University of New South Wales and the University of Technology, Sydney.

We thank the Centre for Cross-Cultural Research for funding the Program; the Department of History, ANU, for subsidising the publication of the book; the Humanities Research Centre, ANU, for provision of its excellent facilities; and Bain Attwood and Wendy Perkins at Monash Publications in History for support in the publishing process.

Others we wish to thank include Kate McCarthy for research and editorial assistance, John Docker for assistance in developing some of the 'Writing History' courses upon which this one was based, and Anne-Maree O'Brien for administrative support at the Centre for Cross-Cultural Research. For their contributions to the Visiting Scholars Program, we warmly thank the following: Robyne Bancroft, Roger Benjamin, Iain McCalman, the late Dymphna Clark, Claire Haywood, Marian Quartly, Paul Tapsell, Burgmann College, ANU, Environment ACT, and Nancy Sever, Director of the Drill Hall Gallery at the ANU. We thank Mandy Martin for permission to reproduce a detail from one of her paintings for the cover of this book.

We also wish to thank Bain Attwood, Marie Pernat, Jo Bramble, James Cannon, Sarah Cannon, Kathy Lothian and Joanne Mullins for the work they did to ensure the publication of the new edition of this book.

PREFACE TO THE ELECTRONIC EDITION

We are delighted that Monash University ePress is republishing *Writing Histories: Imagination and Narration* as a print and an e-book. Electronic publication will enable it to reach a larger audience. We are grateful to Monash Publications in History for publishing the book in the first place. Since that time, it has reached a diverse audience. This is so, we think, because there are few books quite like this one. There are many guides to writing history essays and theses, and to writing particular kinds of history—family, local, church, and company history, to mention those most likely to attract writing guides—but there are few that aim to assist in the writing of general and academic histories. We hope this republication assists a new generation of budding historians to participate in the adventure of mind and imagination that is the writing of history.

We have updated the reading guide and bibliography to include material published since the book's first edition. In Australia and internationally, the discipline has undergone many significant changes since 2000, including the 'history wars', the debates around history and fiction prompted by Kate Grenville's *The Secret River*, and the moves towards transnational history. The reading guide now includes some of the main texts from these developments. It also has several books that have appeared since their authors reflected in this volume on the writing challenges they presented.

Finally, we note with great sadness the passing of one of our contributors, Greg Dening, in 2008. Greg had a long and distinguished career as an historian of international reputation, but we knew him mainly towards the end of his career, when he conducted many workshops for PhD students at the Australian National University and elsewhere. He inspired his students, and indeed his peers, to have faith in their projects, believe in the value of history generally, realise that historical writing is always a performance, and aim high in their writing. We dedicate this electronic edition of *Writing Histories: Imagination and Narration* to him.

Ann Curthoys
Sydney, February 2009

Ann McGrath
Canberra, February 2009

INTRODUCTION

Ann Curthoys
Ann McGrath

This collection of essays is designed to help anyone wanting to write histories that capture the imagination and challenge the intellect. In an effort to uncover the mystery of what it is that makes some histories fascinating and others rather dull, nine historians reflect here on their own practice as writers. All work in Australia and most write in the field of Australian history, but the ideas, techniques and reflections can be applied to any kind of history, written anywhere.

For historians today, both those starting out and those experienced in the older habits of unselfconscious 'writing up', there are many difficult and interesting writing questions to be faced. This book explores some of the most common: how to get started, how to find a 'voice', how to enliven a description or a narration, where to write, how to keep going, and finally how to know when to stop.

There are innumerable 'how to' books for hopeful and practising fiction writers, with advice on questions of plot, character and style, and on how to publish and market your work. There are also many guides to thesis-writing for Honours, Masters and PhD students, whose work forms a major part of historical research and writing today. In addition, there is a flourishing genre in which historians reflect on their work, methods, analysis, intentions, and approach to history.[1] There are, however, few books focussing on problems of form and writing in history, or in which historians reflect *as writers* on their work. History students in universities are taught how to construct a good written argument; essay questions are devised to assess how well they can digest, synthesise, and test a hypothesis. Students are, however, rarely taught ways in which to make their work exciting, dramatic, moving.

This neglect of the intricacies and techniques of the specific art of historical writing springs from the idea that while fiction writers can allow free play for the imagination, history writers are confined by their commitment to historical truth. In this mode of thinking, there is no point worrying about questions of plot and character and point of view, for the historian cannot invent, and must simply write about what he or she finds in the records. There is no real art in history-writing, except to be clear and straightforward, and perhaps well-paced. Thus history writers will tend to see themselves as historians rather than as writers, as 'writing *up*' their research rather than as imaginative and creative writers out to capture the interest of an audience.

WRITING HISTORIES (2009) **MONASH UNIVERSITY EPRESS**

In our view, a more helpful way of thinking about history-writing is to see it as seeking one kind of truth, while fiction seeks another. In both cases, forms of writing must be found to suit the writer's purposes, and in both cases it is important to write well—to inspire, entice, inform, to draw the reader into an adventure of thought.

Our interest in the specifics of history-writing—in questions of technique, form, and creativity—is part of a broader change of mood amongst historians. Under the influence of postmodernism, or the 'linguistic turn', many historians have been drawn to seeing historical documents and sources as texts, whose meaning must be deciphered in the context of an understanding of intertextuality, genre and discourse. In this atmosphere of heightened sensitivity to textuality, many historians have become more conscious of the texts they themselves create. Most influential in this recognition (or more properly rediscovery) of historical writing *as* writing, as a form of creativity and textuality, has been the work of Hayden White.[2] In works such as *Tropics of Discourse* and *The Content of the Form*, White has explored the ways in which historians tell stories. Events, he says, are made into a story by processes of suppression or subordination, which highlight characterisation, motific repetition, variation of tone and point of view, and descriptive strategies—that is, by a variety and armoury of story-telling techniques. The relationships that *appear* to be inherent in the objects inhabiting the field have been imposed by the investigator.[3] Historians, White says, place their historical information in plot-structures that arise from the accumulated conventions of story-telling, not from the events them-selves. The problem is, they rarely realise this is what they are doing. It is a 'fiction' of historians that what they constitute as the beginning or the end of their story are all *real* beginnings or endings, rather than literary constructions.

One does not have to adopt fully White's particular theory of story-telling—he outlines a limited number of main story-types, such as tragedy, comedy, romance, satire and epic—to take his key point: that historians, in constructing an historical narrative, are writing *narrative*. They are deciding what story to tell, and their material offers much more than one possibility. Yet White's emphasis on the constructedness of historical writing has proved controversial, enraging many historians who prefer to emphasise the histories they discover rather than those they create. White has, however, inspired many others, who recognise in his work a description of their own experience of deciding how to tell their story from the historical material they have collected.

White's emphasis on history as story-telling is, of course, not at all new. History was once very conscious of itself as a story-telling craft, and eighteenth-century historians prided themselves on their style, happy to foreground their role as authors, story-tellers and writers. It was only later, under the influence of nineteenth-century desires for science, and with it a single version of the facts—the past, the 'truth'—that the notion of the art of writing tended to fade from historians' consciousness and desires. The leading advocate of history as a science in the nineteenth century was German historian Leopold von Ranke. Ranke was appalled by Walter Scott's extremely popular historical novels, especially their historical inventions, and he resolved in his own work to avoid all imagination and restrict himself severely to the facts, to show only what actually happened. By the end of the century the split between history and literature had become an orthodoxy among professional historians. History, proclaimed the Professor of History at Cambridge, J.B. Bury, in his inaugural lecture in 1903, 'is a science, no less and no more ... History is not a branch of literature'.[4]

In the twentieth century this divorce from an interest in the art of story-telling was further strengthened by the influence of structuralism, with people as diverse as Lewis Namier, R.H. Tawney and Fernand Braudel arguing that it was the duty of historians to analyse structures rather than narrate events. In the 1980s, however, under the influence of post-structuralist critiques of the notion of 'structure' itself, events, and with them narrative, began to make a comeback. Many historians sought to avoid the opposition between structure and event altogether, preferring to investigate particular events for what they reveal about the social structure and the culture in which they took place.[5] With this renewed emphasis on events, and the greater claims made for them as windows on the past, there had to be greater attention to the arts of description and narration, and to drawing connections between the particular and the general.

There also had to be attention to technical issues such as 'voice' and point of view, matters familiar to writers of fiction but less so to writers of history. The most difficult of these questions was that of what kind of authorial voice to adopt. Should one do the usual thing and write in an impersonal 'third person' way, acting as a hidden narrator who knows everything that happened and the reasons it happened the way it did, but never show one's own face? This, after all, is what most of us were taught to do at school and university: never use 'I', history students have been told for generations, and in many cases are still told 'we are not interested in you, only in the story you tell'. As Tom Griffiths remarks in this volume, 'using the personal pronoun is seen to be self-indulgent and unscholarly'. The advice to avoid 'I' fits well with the desire to 'sound objective'. We all know well the kind of history thus produced, and anyone who has written a history essay, thesis, or article knows how to write this way.

Should one venture into more personalised interactive territory, unafraid to say 'I' when necessary, mixing the usual third person narrative style with a first person discussion of the processes of research and interpretation? In postmodern histories, there is a return to the use of 'I', to foregrounding the twists and turns of historical research and the fact of multiple possible interpretations. There is, that is to say, a return to an emphasis on the uncertainty of our knowledge about the past, and on the ways in which our conceptions of the past are embedded in our present. Using 'I' thus reminds the reader that this history has an author, and has involved a myriad of choices and selections at every step. It is also a means of creating interest; the 'I' voice is very powerful, as the popularity and accessibility of autobiography and oral history attests. The return to 'I' thus signifies a desire to engage with popular audiences, to recognise that to narrate is also to perform. The authors in this book do not all agree on the return of the 'I', Bill Gammage in particular regarding it as unnecessary and intrusive, and the avoidance of 'I' as indicating an appropriate historical humility. In his case he aims 'not to intrude into the story', or rather 'not to make intrusion obvious, to let the story unfold as seemingly it did at the time'. Ann McGrath draws attention both to the possibilities of the 'I', and the ways in which its overuse or misuse can have the opposite effect to that intended.

A related issue is the discussion by some authors of ways in which to convey multiple perspectives. Many historians now want to show that the past looked very different to different actors at the time, and since. In this volume Donna Merwick draws our attention to Walter Benjamin's critique of history as a story of progress, and his attention to those who, 'amid the "deafening" voices of the victors, are reduced to silence'. How are we to convey this multiplicity of voices, and how can we leave some interpretative work to the reader, without becoming hopelessly indecisive and confusing? Various techniques have been explored. One approach is that of Caribbean historian Richard Price in his book, *Alabi's World*, and in parts of his later book, *The Convict and the Colonel*, where different points of view are represented with a different type face.[6] In his essay 'History of Events and the Revival of Narrative', Peter Burke suggests that historians still have a great deal to learn from the great modernist novelists like James Joyce, with their experimentation with various forms of narration. Historians, he suggests, could learn to play with chronology and sequence, as Aldous Huxley did in *Eyeless in Gaza*, or with multiple points of view, like Lawrence Durrell in *The Alexandria Quartet*. Yet not all novelistic techniques, such as 'stream of consciousness', he warns, are open to the historians.[7]

Greg Dening suggests that we see writing as a kind of performance, intended to be read aloud and in public, as well as silently and privately. In the spirit of the old adage 'show, don't tell', he urges history writers that their 'story-telling should be so skilful that we don't have to say what it means ... If we go to the theatre, we don't expect the playwright to appear on the stage and tell us what the play means'. Narrative and analysis should be blended together. Dening also gives some very practical advice, as in his suggestion to avoid quoting in indented paragraphs, as people don't read them, and instead of writing captions to illustrations, to 'wrap them around with discursive texts ... [to] make image essays'. He also emphasises the importance of rewriting, both the individual sentence and the entire manuscript.

One major influence on historical discussion of questions of form has been James Clifford and George E. Marcus' collection, *Writing Culture: The Poetics and Politics of Ethnography*, in which they draw attention to the narrative shape of modern ethnographies, where the ethnographer appears as the hero of his (or her) own tale, the discoverer of the secrets of another culture.[8] In response, some anthropologists have experimented with other forms of writing, foregrounding the particular context of their ethnographic research, and the processes through which they came to the understandings they did. Ethnography now had to be written not for an 'objective' and unmarked outside world, but in such a way that its subjects might read and interrogate it. Some historians realised that they too often write like Clifford and Marcus' ethnographers, asserting their mastery over the entire society they describe, hiding their own processes of research, reflection and interpretation. Using historical rather than fieldwork materials for their sources, some historians wish to adopt the methods of postmodern ethnography.

One of our contributors, the anthropologist and historian Deborah Bird Rose, goes a little further, not only applying to history some ideas from postmodern ethnography but also reflecting on the way in which her own ethnographic research in the Victoria River District led her to explore questions of place, time and history. She discusses how, in writing *Hidden Histories*, she sought 'a complex weaving of voices and subject positions', and a subject position for herself that was dialogical and open-ended.[9] In her book, *Country of the Heart*, she works with several narrative strands, including her own text, her Aboriginal co-authors' strand, and her photographer's strand.

For many new writers, and even for experienced ones, the hardest task is to start, to find the voice, style, purpose, and argument that will sustain the historical text they are creating. Inspiration for writing history can come from many sources. Peter Read explores music as a model for writing, in particular the 'fantasy', a free but brief improvisation popular in the Elizabethan age. He is fascinated by Purcell's fantasy for five viols, 'Upon One Note', for its balanced form, emotional peaks, exuberance, compression and elegance.

John Docker describes the process whereby his *1492: The Poetics of Diaspora* moved from 'a mere gleam in its creator's eye' to a completed book. His intellectual journey moves from Said to Joyce, Sir Walter Scott to Walter Benjamin, and he aims to 'to take risks, make sideways moves, go over the top and keep going, journey deep within oneself. One has to cultivate method as a kind of art of madness'.

In trying to find new ways to write history, some historians have had to think more deeply about literary techniques, the creation of interest and understanding via figures of speech such as metaphor, metonymy and simile. Where literary critics track these rhetorical figures in literary texts as a matter of course, historians have little in their training to help them recognise, much less self-consciously use, such techniques. Which is not to say they don't use figures of speech. Metaphor, as Anthony Easthope has shown, is used by historians all the time — to imply social fluidity or rigidity, fast or slow moving historical change, mechanical or organic forms of connectedness, and the like.[10] But they use them unwittingly, with little understanding of the ambiguity and intertextuality of metaphors — as if the metaphor pins down a meaning rather than multiplying the possible meanings of any statement. A clearer understanding of the nature and effects of metaphor might help historians write in more engaging and complex ways. Historians do the same thing in their use of allegory and the anecdote, deploying them unselfconsciously and unreflectively. Very often, in looking for beginnings and origins, they are telling particular kinds of creation stories, with all the features of these, whether religious or scientific, but they do not recognise or understand the nature of the genre within which they work. Knowledge of genre, figures of speech, and rhetorical traditions can help us all become more skilled writers.

It was with issues like these in mind that we ran a three-week course for PhD students in history and related fields in April 1999. The course was funded by the Centre for Cross-Cultural Research at the Australian National University, who paid the students' fares and accommodation in Canberra. Fourteen students from around the country — from Perth, Darwin, Sydney, Melbourne, Wollongong and Canberra — attended the course. In the first week we raised the theoretical and aesthetic questions alluded to above, and many others. We also set some 'loosening up' writing exercises, two of them based on visits to art galleries, inviting students to take a painting as a starting point for writing. In the middle week, students concentrated on their own writing for their theses, and attended talks by practising historians, many of them reproduced here. In the final week, the students' work was workshopped intensively. At the same time, there was a number of excursions to the bush and lakes around Canberra.

The students' reaction was extraordinarily positive. PhD students are often extremely isolated and have very little opportunity to discuss their work in detail with others. They have even less opportunity to discuss the huge writing task that lies before them, to see the writing task as a form of creative writing that can be pleasurable as well as somewhat painful, so large and unfamiliar as the task is for most. A collective enterprise, in which their own and similar writing tasks became the focus of discussion, provided many with new insights and new impetus. In their journals and short exercises, they wrote comments like the following:

> *Sue Hardisty*: I am relieved the first week is over. I feel exhausted and exhilarated. I want to wallow in the lingering sensation of the first week's immersion ritual. A sea of words sweeping over me and a wave of voices whispering, the same message in exciting ways ... 'form needs to be challenged to write a different history'. I feel I have permission to speak ... to explore ways of writing history.

> *Bill Wilson* (at the end of one writing exercise): I would not normally write in such a way. This piece is totally free of my normal writing styles and conventions. In the context of the program and a desire to experiment I have taken a risk.

> *Unknown*: Tom [Griffiths] made the point that historians are also writers. Had to stop and think about that for a minute, but he is right, must remember the point.

> *Bernie Brian*: As a student from a smaller regional university, I feel the biggest disadvantage we have is a limited contact with the larger community of scholars ... While I had always considered myself a reasonable writer, I had never considered myself to be 'a writer' ... The [Visiting Scholars Program] has both inspired me and given me the confidence to redefine myself as a writer and for the first time to see that there may be life after the PhD ... The most important ideas that I took away with me were to not be shy about writing my 'book' creatively and to let my sources speak for themselves. I always felt I needed to come up with some holistic, authoritative, single meaning for my subject matter. In short, I feel I no longer have to be afraid of contradiction ... I came away with a decision to describe and analyse

the events associated with my historical subject, without the overriding urge to make connections that may not even exist.

Ann Standish: My academic training insists that I make clear the connections between the several trains of thought that have travelled through this piece ... my academic training is also screaming out against not only the use of the first person narrator, but also against allowing it to dominate the narrative. I fear an audience will find it dull, indulgent, lacking in internal coherence, and probably too long. I regret that I haven't written something more experimental, more amusing, more entertaining, less earnest. But now it is too late.

Michael Adams: Words can only be one part of how I describe the places in my work. Linking the words with maps, photographs, other images — within the limitations of an academic work — is an unresolved challenge. I'd like my thesis to look like a John Wolsley painting: maps, sketches, illuminating diary notes, diagrams, detail studies, broad landscapes, all combined in one huge and arresting composition that you can explore close-up and also understand in its unified totality.

While residential courses like this one are expensive, non-residential courses can be offered in any city with a significant number of students or others writing history. We hope this book will be useful for people wanting to offer similar courses, whether at universities or in community colleges of various kinds. With this aim in mind, we have included, alongside the chapters in which historians discuss their own writing practices, two further chapters intended for the teacher or the self-managed history-writing group. 'How to workshop your writing' explains how to set up and manage supportive writing environments, equipping history writers with friendly critics who can enrich and empower their writing, and help them realise goals from which they might otherwise shy away. 'Gallery, museum and other exercises for writing history' describes techniques we have used ourselves, which students have found useful.

Many PhD students, and many historians, however, will continue to write in relative isolation. This book is also intended for them. Those writing alone may find the 'Reading guide and bibliography' at the end of the book especially useful. Finally, while many readers may wish to read the chapters 'magpie fashion', they do follow sequentially and are best read in the order they have been presented.

ENDNOTES

1   We list some of these books in the reading guide and bibliography at the end of the book.

2   See especially his *Metahistory: The Historical Imagination in Nineteenth Century Europe*, Johns Hopkins University Press, Baltimore, 1973; *Tropics of Discourse: Essays in Cultural Criticism*, Johns Hopkins University Press, Baltimore, 1978; and *The Content of the Form: Narrative Discourse and Historical Representation*, Johns Hopkins University Press, Baltimore, 1987.

3   H. White, 'The Literary Text as Literary Artifact', in R. Canary and H. Kozicki (eds), *The Writing of History: Literary Form and Historical Understanding*, University of Wisconsin Press, Madison, 1978, pp. 41–62, especially pp. 45–49.

4   J.B. Bury, *Selected Essays of J.B. Bury*, edited H. Temperley, Cambridge University Press, Cambridge, 1930, p. 4.

5   P. Burke, 'History of Events and the Revival of Narrative', in P. Burke (ed.), *New Perspectives on Historical Writing*, Polity Press, Cambridge, 1991, pp. 234–37.

6   R. Price, *Alabi's World*, Johns Hopkins University Press, Baltimore, 1990; *The Convict and the Colonel*, Beacon Press, Boston, 1998.

7   Burke, 'History of Events', pp. 237–40.

8   J. Clifford and G.E. Marcus (eds), *Writing Culture: The Poetics and Politics of Ethnography*, University of California Press, Berkeley, 1986.

9   D. Rose, *Hidden Histories: Black Stories from Victoria River Downs, Humbert River and Wave Hill Stations*, Aboriginal Studies Press, Canberra, 1991.

10 A. Easthope, 'Romancing the Stone: History-Writing and Rhetoric', *Social History*, vol. 18, no. 2, 1993, pp. 235–49.

CHAPTER 1

THE POETICS AND PRACTICALITIES OF WRITING

Tom Griffiths

Inga Clendinnen, an outstanding and imaginative historian, recently confessed that when she asked a class of new history graduates which historians they read for pleasure, they laughed! 'I knew why they laughed', she explained sadly. It's because so many scholars compromise communication with pompous posturing; they are too busy staking out intellectual territory and warding others off it; they are too busy digging in their fields isolating 'stone-hard, stone-cold facts' to bother looking up or around; they are so furiously in pursuit of 'objectivity' that they delete themselves from their scripts and employ a weird, passionless prose. Clendinnen says that she enjoys reading great historians, like E.P. Thompson, for the same reason she enjoys reading great novelists—they offer an entrée into richly imagined worlds. But, she confesses, there is a difference. For her, when reading non-fiction, the bliss is tempered and intensified by a critical alertness and an undertow of moral implication not present in what she calls 'the limpid realms of fiction'.[1]

So, Clendinnen is throwing out a challenge to us. Look how bad, how inward-looking the writing of scholars can be, she says; yet see what heights we, particularly as writers of non-fiction, can reach.

In a marvellous little book entitled *The Writing Life*, the versatile American author Annie Dillard tells a story about how she learned to chop wood. Once, in order to finish a book, she begged the use of a small cabin which was heated with a wood stove and situated on a remote and sparsely populated island in northern Puget Sound, Washington State. It was a beautiful setting, but all she noticed was the cold. At first she did not know how to split wood. She

> set a chunk of alder on the chopping block and harrassed it, at enormous exertion, into tiny wedges that flew all over the sandflat and lost themselves ... After a few whacks my alder chunk still stood serene and unmoved, its base untouched, its tip a thorn.[2]

One night, Annie Dillard had a dream in which she was given to understand how to split wood. 'You aim, said the dream—of course!—at the chopping block ... You cannot do the job cleanly unless you treat the wood as the transparent means to an end, by aiming past it.'[3] You wonder why she is telling this story, until she later reveals it as a parable for writing. I will return to it.

I am interested in the poetics and practicalities of writing. I want to progress from quite general issues about the debilitating and enabling metaphors that govern our writing in universities to more personal stories about the sensualities of writing as an art: What does it feel like to write? What are the sources of good writing? And finally to practical reflections and advice: What do we need to do to write, to make writing a significant and meaningful part of our scholarly lives?

METAPHORS

First, let me say something about the disabling conventions of writing in universities, and how we might confront and subvert them.

Judith Brett, an Australian political scientist and a fine, clear writer (see her book, *Robert Menzies' Forgotten People*), has written a thoughtful and provocative article on 'The Bureaucratisation of Writing'. She wonders 'why so few academics are public intellectuals' and also asks why so few of them are good writers.[4] Brett lists three simple preconditions for good discursive prose. They are: a fully imagined audience, a sense of urgency, and something interesting or important to say. The biggest problem with academic writing, she thinks, is achieving the first two. Most *do* have something important or interesting to say. So what is it that works against them feeling compelled to say it in ways that engage an audience outside their discipline?

Brett argues, and I think she's right, that the modern bureaucratic university has created an environment where it is difficult to take writing seriously, where to devote time to good writing goes against the grain of the job. The corporatisation of universities and the bureaucratisation of writing and knowledge within the academy, she argues, disconnects the university writer from the two traditional sources of energy for good writing and good books: that is, a fully imagined public, and one's own subjectivity. In universities, being a writer who seeks a general audience can invite suspicion; you sometimes hear the words 'popular' and 'paperback' spat out at seminars and selection committees. 'Mere journalism' is beneath us. And using the personal pronoun is seen to be self-indulgent and unscholarly. I recently even had to defend the writing of *books* at my own university; they were evidently seen by some as suspiciously holistic and accessible products. Essays for widely-read newspapers or serious periodicals, however esteemed, are valued much less in the academy than refereed articles for international journals, however obscure. The local, home audience, however large, can be seen as less important than a distant, overseas one, however small. Clear, everyday language can be seen as less scholarly than specialised jargon.

What's going on here? Universities reward us for writing obscurely for distant, small, specialised audiences made up of people educated exactly as we are! As Brett puts it, we are trained to write continually for the approval only of a disciplinary elite, whether we are students handing in essays, doctoral candidates writing a PhD for two or three examiners, or academics writing only for refereed journals. Listen to her devastating critique of this culture, our culture:

> Academic writing is writing that never leaves school, that never grows beyond the judging, persecuting eye of the parent to enter into a dialogue with the society and culture of its time, as an adult amongst other adults, with all the acceptance of mutual imperfection which this implies. Always seeking the approval of a higher authority, the academic writer endlessly defers responsibility. I write in this way because I have to pass the exam, to get my PhD, to get a job, to get tenure, to get promotion. I write like this because it is what *they* want. I don't write in the way best suited to what I have to say, or to win people to a cause, to change the world, to humiliate my opponents, to help people understand their lives, to please my readers, or even to please myself.[5]

So, graduate workshops that place the act of writing itself at the centre of their concerns are radical. They are questioning these hierarchies and pretensions, questioning the twentieth-century university world of social science neutrality, detachment and narrow professionalisation. They forbid us from deferring responsibility. They seek to free us from some of these constraints of our institutional culture, to open our minds to other ways of being scholarly, but they also charge us with the responsibility to find a voice.

Let's be clear about what this means. We don't have to be less theoretical. We don't have to avoid writing for refereed journals. We don't have to cancel our registration for that specialised overseas conference. We mustn't be less thorough in our research nor less humble in the face of our subject. But we do have to avoid using language and status to intimidate, obfuscate or exclude. We do have to acknowledge and stop feeling embarrassed by the power of stories. We do have to stop seeing passion and objectivity as mutually exclusive. And we do have to see writing as an essential and primary part of our work.

Some of the metaphors for university writing work directly against this. One is that you 'write up'. That is, you do all the research, and then you report, you write up. This is the humanities scholar as social scientist. The metaphor is taken directly from the natural and physical sciences, the world of hypothesis and experiment, and it carries with it the implication of detachment and objectivity. That is why you write 'up'. To 'write down' or just plain 'write' suggests something that is much more literary and creative, there is some sense of the power of the writer in it, as recorder, as testifier, as interpreter. 'Writing up', by contrast, is routine, perfunctory.

The metaphor of 'writing up' divides scholarship into two phases, one long, uncertain and exciting—that is, research—and the other short, predetermined and boring—that is, writing. 'Writing up' completes research, it ties off ends. It is uncreative. It is not in dialogue with research; it simply reports on it. It is done quickly, unwillingly and last.

What a debilitating metaphor this is for us scholars for whom the role of language in shaping and probing reality is crucial. Of course scientists, too, work with descriptive metaphors all the time; they grapple continually with contingency and uncertainty. But, in the humanities and social sciences, language is both our means and our subject. It's where you begin, as well as where you end. Let's talk about writing early rather than writing up.

Another disabling metaphor or word for us is 'thesis'. 'Thesis' suggests something arcane before we have even begun, something limited and specialised that will never see the light of day, something that will only ever be bound and gagged. Publishers shudder at the word. I would prefer to talk about our 'books'. That's what we're writing, that's what we hope they might be, that's a word that reminds us that we have to fully imagine an audience.

Another word we have to watch is 'topic'. It may at first seem a benign little word, but it's a time-bomb. The problem with 'topic' is that it enlists a spatial metaphor. It suggests an enquiry that is discrete, tightly bounded and territorial. It carries with it the implication that you define your topic at the start and stick with it; it suggests that one defines one's PhD subject by marking out the boundaries of one's intellectual territory; it suggests that you choose vacant terrain and then constantly boundary-ride to keep it so; it implies that originality is a measure of how virgin is the ground you choose and how deeply you dig it. I utterly reject these implications. Virgin ground is not essential for original research: indeed, a crowded field can be more lively and productive than a vacant one. We should be alert for the relationships between our own work and those of others; the more scholarly conversations we can get into the better. Originality is a many-splendoured thing; it can be measured laterally as well as by depth; it can reside in a scholar's span or powers of synthesis, or perception of relationships beyond the tilled field or across the fourth dimension of time. And a PhD, any book, is a journey—if you don't finish up somewhere different to where you began then you probably haven't learnt much. 'Journey' is an enabling metaphor; it is open-minded and open-ended. On a journey, you creatively construct experience. You discover something about yourself as well as the place and society you are travelling through. It is transformative. There is more room for those chief virtues of curiosity and wonder in the idea of a journey.

Experience, for the historian as much as any writer, is the ultimate primary source. I've always valued those sayings that emphasise that historians—people who are professionally occupied with the past—must nevertheless engage in especially active ways with the present. 'Good historians need strong boots' urged the British socialist historian, R.H. Tawney. 'I would give trainee historians the chance to travel the world', declared Theodore Zeldin. 'I'm an historian—therefore I love life', announced Lucien Febvre. We all write out of our own experience. There has to be a bit of yourself in the writing. That's where you start. What do you use for bait to catch the words and ideas? Dillard says you have no choice, and then tells us a story about an Algonquin woman and her baby who were left alone in their winter camp after everyone else had starved. The woman found one small fishhook. It was simple to rig a line, but she had no bait, and no hope of bait. So she took a knife and cut a strip from her own thigh. 'She fished with the worm of her own flesh and caught a jackfish; she fed the child and herself. Of course she saved the fish gut for bait.' She and her baby survived. The message of the story is clear: the writer must fish with the worm of her own flesh.[6]

Dillard uses other powerful metaphors for writing. They are all active and instrumental. Writing is a tool; it is a journey; it is climbing a ladder into the clouds. Your line of words, she says, is a miner's pick, a woodcarver's gouge, a surgeon's probe, a fibre optic. 'You wield it, and it digs a path you follow. Soon you find yourself deep in new territory.'[7]

My own metaphor for historical research, in spite of being another depth metaphor, is at least a fluid and processual one. It is that of dredging a pond. If the world is a deep pond and we live on the surface, swimming so that we can also breathe, then the historian's job is to dredge the pond, keeping it healthy by continually disturbing the water and its contents. The surface is a busy but—by definition—superficial place, and there is limited room in the limelight at any one time. Things that we once had given favoured attention on the surface later sink into the murky depths, forgotten. Historians dredge, continually dredge. Diving can be scary and hazardous, and you can't afford to stay down too long. But the quest is compelling: to remember, remind, discover, bringing to the surface half-familiar shapes, disturbing the superficial present with evidence from the depths.

Another disabling word is 'definitive'. The problem with 'definitive' is that it introduces a deadening metaphor; it suggests that your aim is to end debate, whereas it is actually the opposite. Your aim is to start it. Your aim is not to dampen down but to stir up; it is not to exhaust but to enliven, not to bury but to unearth. And one rarely unearths things whole; one has to recognise them, reconstitute them, re-imagine them. 'Being definitive' generally means being pedantic and narrowly competitive; it means closing down possibilities rather than opening them up; it means mistaking accuracy for truth; it works against being generous or imaginative or speculative. Remember the poet A.D. Hope's 'macabre academic hero', Dr Budge:

> The scabs scratched off by genius, sought with care
> Stuck back again earn Doctor Budge a chair;
> And now, Professor Budge, his claim made good,
> He works like dry rot through the Sacred Wood;
> Or like dead mackerel, in a night of ink
> Emits a pale gleam and a mighty stink.[8]

I'm sure Professor Budge's scholarship was definitive. This scholarly stance also implies that objectivity is only gained through cool, dispassionate detachment, through emotional distance. But let's believe instead that objectivity comes from breadth of understanding, from humility, from tolerance, and from engagement. The Australian historian Keith Hancock named the three great virtues of an historian as attachment, justice and span, and attachment came first.[9]

But perhaps the most disabling phrase or metaphor of all is that what we write is 'non-fiction'. To call our writing 'non-fiction' seems to deny its creative, imaginative dimensions; it's *not* something, and the something it's not is that rather wonderful and captivating world of fiction. It's also a phrase that seems to turn our backs on stories, because stories are so identified with the realm of fiction. But stories are the stuff of history; they are privileged carriers of truth. The American nature writer Barry Lopez reminds us that truth cannot be reduced to aphorism or formula: 'It is something alive and unpronounceable. Story creates an atmosphere in which truth becomes discernible as a pattern.'[10]

The 'non' in our non-fiction, then, does not need to be a denial or a suppression; rather, it signifies an edge that can sharpen our prose and heighten our sense of danger and wonder. Dillard compares the good writer with the top tennis player—both play the edges, hit up the line. You can't play too safely, too much within the boundaries, or there's no game and no challenge; and if you play too much beyond them, you will offend reason and poetry—and you'll be called out.

Writing true stories is the product of a fascinating struggle between imagination and evidence.[11] That struggle constitutes our discipline. I mean 'discipline' not just in its academic sense; it is what writing is all about, particularly writing non-fiction. Imagination must work in creative friction with a given world, there are rules as well as freedoms, there are hard edges of reality one must respect. There is a world out there that humbles one, disciplines one. There are silences not of our making. Clendinnen worries away at these silences. Much of what we most want to know about the past we cannot know, she says. Or probably cannot know. 'Were this fiction, I would know that all things said and left unsaid, all disruptions, were intended to signify. But this is not fiction, and I cannot be sure.'[12]

It is our job to release reality, enable it to be seen, enable voices and silences to be heard. Let me offer you another metaphor. Writing is a form of sculpture. First one must amass the clay, the raw material of reality, building up the rough form, gathering much more than one can eventually keep. Then begins the careful paring away, the sculpting and moulding, the tweaking out of detail. The final reality emerges, and one could almost believe that it was always there, trapped in the clay, awaiting discovery and rescue. True stories are the best stories. Paradoxically, we must strive to make them believable.

The way you conceive of writing determines how you go about it. So, let's implement the metaphors, and proceed to the practicalities.

PRACTICALITIES

I am now going to consider ways of getting yourself to write. I'm not concerned here with how you write; I'm concerned simply that you write, and that you write early. How do we organise our lives to do this? Where and how does writing happen? There are no right answers to such questions, of course; you have to work out what suits you. All I can offer is some of my own thoughts and experience.

However social and environmental are the sources of writing, I believe that the act itself remains fundamentally and positively lonely. You have to like your own company to be a writer. Writing in public or by committee doesn't work. Writing is, at heart, very private. I won't say anti-social, because I've been impressing on you how social and outgoing it can be, and I'm using words like performing, and audience and conversation, to express that. But I have to say that good writing happens alone. The writer speaks to the reader with a directness and personal intimacy that is both scary and exhilarating and that is born of solitude.

I have been writing about the country back of Bourke in far western New South Wales. I visited it in company with an artist, Mandy Martin. It was my job to write an essay for the catalogue accompanying her next exhibition of paintings. When we were out in the field together, it struck me how similar were our tasks, but how different our products. She stood in front of her landscape and conjured shapes onto the canvas. She splashed and washed colour about, used a bit of the sand at her feet; she deftly sketched in some detail. This was the underpainting, an urgent and fluent capturing of raw material and impressions which she would later refine. Meanwhile, I was sitting on a log on the banks of the Darling River, doing much the same but with words, writing furiously and indiscriminately, throwing onto the paper snatches of conversation with locals, new words I had learnt, brief descriptions of people I'd met or things I'd observed, preparing the ground for later, more considered writing. But the artist's creativity was visible and public and social, the dogs and children played around her feet, an impromptu painting lesson for a nine-year-old was conducted on the side, and the artist had something to show, something to be admired, and the product, even in its unfinished state, was propped up on the homestead table. But after my two hours of uninterrupted silence sitting on a log, I stuffed my pages of scrawl into a bag and took them away with me. I collected a strand of Mitchell grass, and a jar of red sand. They sit on my desk at home as I try to turn that scrawl into something that, one day, might find its way back to the homestead table.[13]

So, writing happens alone, and there is generally a long wait between inspiration and response. You have to be both urgent and patient, urgent enough to get it done and patient enough to await your audience. For big writing tasks, you have to have the focus and sense of occasion to produce something special, but also the stamina and the routine to keep doing it month after month. I find I have to be in a state of controlled panic. Plain panic is no good at all. When it is controlled, it can become an asset, for a short while. It's like nervousness when you are speaking in public, another sort of performing. Uncontrolled nerves are debilitating; you can't remember your words or even read a script. But controlled nervousness is a boon, in fact it's essential. Any performer will tell you this. You need to be keyed up to be properly focussed. The day you worry is the day you are not nervous when you get up to speak in public. It's the same with writing. The day you worry is the day when writing doesn't matter enough to be exciting, or when the audience is so unimportant to you that it cannot be imagined, or when the deadline is so flexible that it does not scare you.

So, you need to contrive to be alone, you need to be in a state of controlled panic, and you need to establish this extraordinary state as a routine! Dillard dramatises this hilariously, with stories of her self-imposed exile in lonely beach shacks, her overdoses of coffee and cigarettes, and her reading aloud of poetry during writing breaks. She summarises the problem beautifully:

> [The writer] must be sufficiently excited to rouse himself to the task at hand, and not so excited he cannot sit down to it. He must have faith sufficient to impel and renew the work, yet not so much faith he fancies he is writing well when he is not.
>
> For writing a first draft requires from the writer a peculiar internal state which ordinary life does not induce. If you were a Zulu warrior banging on your shield with your spear for a couple of hours along with a hundred other Zulu warriors, you might be able to prepare yourself to write. If you were an Aztec maiden who knew months in advance that on a certain morning the priests were going to throw you into a hot volcano, and if you spent those months undergoing a series of purification rituals and drinking dubious liquids, you might, when the time came, be ready to write. But how, if you are neither Zulu warrior nor Aztec maiden, do you prepare yourself, all alone, to enter an extraordinary state on an ordinary morning?[14]

Well, I think the beach shack plan has quite a bit going for it. My wife and I both write, and we plan our calendar to ensure that we each get a few days away on our own to write several times a year. We take it in turns to pack up our notes and books and portable computer and a photograph of the children, the coffee, the wine, and even some food, and go somewhere simple but comfortable—Dillard's beach shack sounds perfect—and you feel really silly if you've put the rest of the family to such inconvenience and then come back with nothing written. It fulfils all the criteria—you're alone, the blank screen and the brevity of the trip ensures that your panic is barely controlled, and if you subject yourself to this regularly then you've made a sort of routine out of the extraordinary.

Coming home is also important. One of the essential requirements of every writer is a sympathetic and constructively critical first reader whose opinion you respect. Relinquishing—and let me dwell on that word—*relinquishing* your draft to a valued reader helps distance yourself from it. No matter what they say, it temporarily passes the responsibility, it helps you find the energy to re-write it, as you inevitably must do. It's nerve-wracking, but it's also such a relief.

Dillard imagines that every morning you climb several flights of stairs, enter your study, open the French doors, and slide your desk and chair out into the middle of the air, floating thirty feet from the ground. Birds fly under your chair. Your work is to drive the engine of belief that keeps you and your desk in mid-air. She describes one of her studies as a pine shed on Cape Cod, eight feet by ten feet: 'Like a plane's cockpit, it is crammed bulkhead to bulkhead with high-tech equipment. All it needs is an altimeter; I never quite know where I am.' 'Appealing workplaces are to be avoided', she claims. 'One wants a room with no view, so imagination can meet memory in the dark.'[15] She pushes her desk against a blank wall where she cannot see from any window. I cannot agree with her; I need a horizon.

One of my favourite historians, Eric Rolls, when at his farm in northern New South Wales, always wrote with his back to a broad window. 'The imagination works better against a blank wall', he says. But the sun on his back warms him, reminds him of the outside world he is trying to capture on paper. Of his Silky Oak desk, he says: 'everything on it knows its place. Words come to it that I am not expecting.' His desk is like a museum of a distant technological era. On it are a pile of handwritten notebooks, eleven dictionaries and books of words, and a typed outline of the current book. He adds five new pages of writing to the pile each day. Empty blocks of lined A4 paper sit beside him, and the two fountain pens that have written all his books. In front of him is a large, disconcerting pile of letters that need answering. There's a big splinter of fragrant sandalwood, a tail feather from a Swamp Pheasant, little soapstone turtles from China, a branding iron and two blocks of Mulga.[16]

Greg Dening writes of his 'desk overlooking Bass Strait'. He peddles in mid-air looking out to sea. In one of his books he tells us that he expected to see a replica of the *Bounty* sail past from that desk, one of the 'Tall Ships' voyaging to Sydney for Australia's bicentenary.[17] There he was, perched in his coastal eyrie, suspended amongst the gums, waiting for the ship—the ship of his imagination—to float on the horizon as if conjured there by his historical gaze. How much coffee had he been drinking?

Charles Dickens went for a long walk across London every afternoon. He found his stories in the faces of the people he passed in the street. In Paris, he found he couldn't write. His pen dried up whenever he was stranded from his city, his source.

THE POETICS AND PRACTICALITIES OF WRITING **CHAPTER 1**

Where do you work? How do you drive the engine of belief? What is your source? Take careful note of the things that help you write, or that help you feel good about writing, and cultivate them. You need to trick yourself into writing, almost by accident. You need to persuade yourself to write, reward yourself for writing. Don't wait for the lightning to strike or the light bulb to switch on in your head. Magical things do happen when you write, but they are generally a product of your sustained wrestling with words. So you have to get to it. The inventor Thomas Edison said his genius was ten per cent inspiration and ninety per cent perspiration. The single thing that most differentiates writers and non-writers is not necessarily that writers are more gifted with words but simply that writers work at it every day through the years of their lives. I sometimes think that, just as the difference between a good haircut and a bad haircut is one week, so the difference between a good writer and a bad writer is two drafts.

If you think writing's hard, then try *not* writing! Fran Lebowitz worked for twelve years on the first chapter of her next novel. She had a ten-year writer's block. This is what she had to say in an interview in *The Paris Review*:

> *What did you do during those years?*
>
> I sulked. Sulking is a big effort. So is not writing. I only realised that when I did start writing. When I started getting real work done I realised how much easier it is to write than not to write. Not writing is probably the most exhausting profession I've ever encountered. It takes it out of you … Not writing is more of a psychological problem than a writing problem. All the time I'm not writing, I feel like a criminal. Actually, I suppose that's probably an outmoded phrase because I don't think criminals feel like criminals any more. I feel like criminals used to feel when they felt guilty about being criminals, when they regretted their crimes. It's horrible to feel felonious every second of the day. Especially when it goes on for years. It's much more relaxing actually to work.
>
> Still, I don't get nearly the amount of work done that I read other people do. This is what most interests me in interviews with writers. I'm not interested in the thoughts or ideas of these people. I only want to know how many pages a day they wrote. If I could meet Shakespeare, I would ask: 'What time did you get up? Do you write at night?' I don't know many writers. I don't have many friends who

are writers. But as soon as I meet any, as soon as I can figure out that it's not too intimate a question to ask them, which is about six seconds after I meet them, I say: 'How many words do you write a day?'[18]

How do you measure a task like writing? Writing a book takes so long that you have to break it into manageable, completable sections. You have to feel you've achieved your day's or week's goal, and then relax, let it go. You can't maintain a controlled panic for long. Counting words is useful, partly because it reminds you just how small your daily goal is. Thomas Mann was an incredibly productive writer. He wrote a page a day. A page a day, 365 pages a year. That's a good sized book every year.[19] That's unusual. And don't forget that some days you throw out what you wrote the day before, and that throwing out their own words is one of the most creative things writers do. Dillard estimates that full-time writers might be lucky to average a usable fifth of a page a day.

I find that writing short essays helps me approach the bigger task. It gets me writing early; it gives me a job I can finish; and it begins my journey towards the book. I also recommend that, if you accept that you need to write early, and that you're taking a journey rather than filling out a topic, then you need to keep a travel diary. You need to record where you've come from. Your story is not only what you are seeing on the way, but how you yourself have changed along the journey. So I think you need to keep a journal of a kind, or else adopt a note-taking system that records the time and place and temper of your notes. Databases can dissipate this context away. But that's your unique story, that's your historiography.

Footnotes and references are an essential part of the art. They are sometimes seen as heavily pretentious scholarly baggage. They are sometimes seen as self-justificatory. They are sometimes seen as old-fashioned. But I'm intrigued by the number of readers who dig into them—they recognise them as an archaeology of knowledge, a labyrinthine journey into other possible worlds, other possible visions. Footnotes are supremely postmodern in the way they annotate and sometimes undermine the authorial voice; they splinter the superficiality of the page, the linearity of the narrative. They are hard-copy hypertext, offering opportunities for readers to find their own paths through the same material. They are not boastful but actually humble, for they make one vulnerable; they offer signposts for others to follow; they empower your readers to arrive at different conclusions.

Computers have changed the way we write, and the way we talk about writing. The word processor has freed us up to be more sculptural in our sense of what sort of craft writing is. One can truly shape a manuscript. One is tempted to be more playful and experimental. The wonder of looking at historic literary manuscripts today is to confront their materiality and linearity. Patrick White wrote his novels right through three times. I think the danger of the word processor, with its cut and paste dexterity, is to fool us that we can do without this linearity, continuity and momentum. In the end, the words still have to be read from left to right.

We have focussed right onto the page or the screen now, and this is where I've been heading and where I want to end. Counting words, working out what goes above or below the footnote line, putting one word in front of another; this is where you end up if you've contrived to be alone, if you've committed the time to write early, if you're peddling at your favourite desk in mid-air with a jar of red sand sitting in front of you—your sympathetic first reader awaits your words, you're controlling the panic … then the page confronts you. This is where it all happens.

I began with Dillard's intriguing parable about chopping wood. 'Who will teach me to write?' a reader wanted to know of her. The page, the page, that eternal blankness, the page in its purity of possibilities; that page, says Dillard, will teach you to write. 'There is another way of saying this', she continues. 'Aim for the chopping block. If you aim for the wood, you will have nothing. Aim past the wood, aim through the wood; aim for the chopping block.'[20]

Have you decided what she means by this? Perhaps it has many meanings. For me, it means: you will discover what you want to say, and how to say it, through the writing process itself. You don't have to come ready and finished to the page. You are not 'writing up'. You come to the page prepared to explore, to imagine, to journey. It is your workshop, your office, your chopping block. Your words will be like splintered wood, the casual by-product of your engagement with the page. Good luck!

ENDNOTES

[1] I. Clendinnen, 'Fellow Sufferers: History and Imagination', *Australian Humanities Review*, 1997–98, electronic journal at http://www.lib.latrobe.edu.au/AHR.

[2] Dillard, *The Writing Life*, Pan Books, London, 1990, pp. 41–43. Reprinted by the permission of Russell & Volkening, Inc., as agents for the author. Copyright © 1989 by Annie Dillard.

[3] *Ibid*., pp. 41–43.

[4] J. Brett, 'The Bureaucratisation of Writing: Why So Few Academics are Public Intellectuals', *Meanjin*, vol. 50, no. 4, 1991, pp. 513–22; *Robert Menzies' Forgotten People*, Macmillan, Sydney, 1992.

[5] Brett, pp. 521–22.

6   Dillard, *The Writing Life*, pp. 12–13.

7   *Ibid.*, p. 3.

8   A.D. Hope, *Dunciad Minor*, Melbourne University Press, Carlton, 1970, p. 36. Reproduced by arrangement with the licensor, The Estate of A.D. Hope, C/- Curtis Brown (Aust) Pty Ltd. W.K. Hancock describes Budge as a 'macabre academic hero' (and quotes from the poem) in his *Professing History*, Sydney University Press, Sydney, 1976, p. 20.

9   Hancock, *Professing History*, chapter 1.

10   B. Lopez, *Crossing Open Ground*, Macmillan, London, 1988, p. 69.

11   Janet McCalman writes superbly about this struggle in 'Translating Social Inquiry into the Art of History', *Tasmanian Historical Studies*, vol. 5, no. 1, 1995–96, pp. 4–15.

12   Clendinnen, 'Fellow Sufferers'.

13   It did. The essay, 'The Outside Country: An Elemental History', is published in M. Martin *et al.*, *Watersheds: The Paroo to the Warrego*, Mandy Martin/Goanna Print, Canberra, 1999, pp. 39–54. The exhibition and publication were launched in Swan Hill, Mildura, Bathurst and Newcastle.

14   Dillard, *The Writing Life*, pp. 46–47. Reprinted by the permission of Russell & Volkening, Inc., as agents for the author. Copyright © 1989 by Annie Dillard.

15   *Ibid.*, p. 26.

16   E. Rolls, *Doorways: A Year of the Cumberdeen Diaries*, Angus & Robertson, Sydney, 1989, pp. 145–47.

17   G. Dening, *Mr Bligh's Bad Language: Passion, Power and Theatre on the Bounty*, Cambridge University Press, Cambridge, 1992, p. 4.

18   An extract from this interview was published in the *Age*, 13 November 1993, under the heading 'On Not Writing'. Reproduced courtesy of The Wylie Agency, Inc.

19   I have drawn this example from Dillard, *The Writing Life*, p. 14.

20   *Ibid.*, p. 59.

THE BROKEN YEARS: AUSTRALIAN SOLDIERS IN THE GREAT WAR 1914–18

Bill Gammage

I've been asked to talk on my thesis, 'The Broken Years', which I wrote at the ANU in 1967–70, and particularly to mention aspects which might help you. You know the basic rules, so I'll talk about what to say. Every topic and set of sources has its own challenges and opportunities, but I urge you from the beginning to think constantly about what you want to say, and to ensure that what you say rises from and above your sources to comment on the human condition. Your thesis only begins as a sequence of well re-searched and arranged sources. No less than literature, art and music, it should end by having significance arching above your topic.[1]

My interest in Australia in the 1914–18 war began in High School, when a country town memorial made me curious about what Australians had endured then. Later I was shown soldiers' letters in the Australian War Memorial. The war emerged as a major event of which I knew nothing, and which no history I took mentioned. I wanted to read more on it, and more of those letters, and my honours and postgraduate theses were chances to do so.

It took me much longer to find what to say. I began work during the Vietnam War, which reinforced my early belief that Australia's Official Historian of 1914–18, C.E.W. Bean, was 'pro-war'. But at last Bean's wonderfully sympathetic detail and the letters made me see that I should focus not on the war, at least not overtly, but on the men who fought it. Their lives were changed forever, and on such a scale that the impact on Aus-tralia and the world was immeasurable.

So I wanted to depict a tragedy—for individuals, for Australia, for the world. Some military historians have said that my work merely imitates Bean's. I doubt that he would have thought so. He wrote an epic, an account of the character of Australian manhood during its greatest trial. I hoped to write of a terrible loss, a catastrophe which changed Australia forever.

How might a thesis say this? The Great War was a tragedy at many levels. It destroyed monarchies, individuals, classes, ways of life. In Australia it changed the direction of society. 'The Broken Years' is fundamentally about why Australia after 1918 was so vastly different from Australia before 1914. Yet the soldiers' letters convinced me that I should centre on the individuals who most endured the war: front-line soldiers. I saw them as civilians, caught in a momentous event certainly, but no less citizens than we.

My first task became to understand why they did what they did. That would teach me something about what remains the same, and what differs, between generations in Australia. In turn, that would convey larger themes about Australia, war, change and loss.

I began on the wrong tack. I wrote a draft of roughly 60 000 words, arranged by stages in a soldier's experience: Before the First Battle, The First Battle, After and so on. While my supervisor, Bruce Kent, was reading this draft, I saw that it left unclear something vital to tragedy: a confrontation between man and circumstance. It showed neither how very great are the pressures needed to force someone to change long-held beliefs, nor how often in the end the war was great enough to force this change. The process was cumulative, not episodic. So the story had to be chronological, relentlessly intensifying the physical and psychological pressure, reaching a point where if the soldiers survived, their world changed, and they brought home new outlooks and ways.

Circumstance, for example, made soldiers more fatalistic—as reading their letters made me. They grew less and less able to think that they might have a say in what happened to them. Usually this point sits in the shadows of my writing, but occasionally I signal it directly (xvii), and sometimes I reinforce it stylistically. When describing the fighting after the Landing at Anzac, I write that exhausted men were forced to fight battle after battle in unwearying succession (58). There is a similar reference in the account of each of the battles which had greatest mental impact on the AIF (see for example 163).

Greek tragedy is the obvious model for a tragedy of man and circumstance. In the later writing stages the model influenced me, just as classical Greece inspired and consoled so many of the architects, sculptors, artists and poets who commemorated the Great War. There was the terrible irony of those pre-war ideals, so loud, so confident, so certain, coming to such ruin; and there was the tragedy of so many individuals who, because they were ready to defend what they cherished, were not only led to misery, pain and death, but took to destruction the very society they held dear. They made their own desert. From the beginning we know this happened: a Greek sense of tragic inevitability cannot escape anyone looking back on 1914–18.

A Greek model seemed apt for another reason. Politicians during the Vietnam War talked much as they had in 1914–18. I knew they wouldn't deliver; I saw that Vietnam veterans would be disillusioned as those of 1918 were. The same script was being acted out. As the Greeks knew well, people never learn, or in time forget. The mistakes of our ancestors are those we can make.

Greek tragedy echoes through 'The Broken Years'. The thesis has a Prologue and Epilogue. It begins 'There never was a greater tragedy than World War I', and I hope there is a sense of men's ideals leading them inescapably to misery. The picture of men going so cheerfully or so resolutely to such catastrophe is terrible, as Homer shows in writing of Troy, on the other side of the Dardanelles from Anzac.

Yet the model was inapt in three ways. First, it suggested how Australian soldiers might reflect the universal and eternal, but I was also interested in the local and particular—the Anzac tradition, in what ways Australians became different from their forebears, how being Australian was expressed in war. Second, these men fell less far than did the Greek heroes, because they began less high, and perhaps less proud. Third, for the AIF not all was ruin. Some ideals survived: notions of manhood, of mateship, of the toughness of life and how little you can expect from it, and so on. These adapted certainly, but they were not ruined. On the contrary the war offered them resurrection, as for example when the post-war Returned Servicemen's League so firmly supported that Empire for which its members suffered so much. The signs are there in 1914 that Imperial sentiment might have waned in Australian much sooner but for the war.

This kind of adaptation, of resurrection, is Christian, not Greek. Greek gods would never have let mortals off the hook like that. Sooner or later, usually at the moment of ruin, they made people see the consequences of their own inadequacies. For Greek historians, it is true, life did not always come to that: whereas the dramatists wanted to say how people should suffer for folly, the historians were constrained to say how they did suffer.

So my thesis parted from a Greek model, to tell of a reluctant but inexorable adaptation by men to circumstances of their own creating, which they lost the power and will to control (if they ever had it), but from which, like Bean, they took at least consolation, and sometimes new purpose and affirmation.

The Greek historians were also dramatists. All historians have a view of what has happened. Thus they cannot know what it is like not to know. Yet a historian's primary task is to say what it was like. This paradox is one reason why art and the past can never be the same, and why for historians art must above all convey a true sense of what was. The greatest Greek historian, Thucydides, achieved this by having a hero, Pericles, who typified and spoke the great virtues, but whose fatal flaws explained the ruin of Athens without diminishing his moral stature. This was a device, but it met the immense responsibility Thucydides had to tell the future what those times were like, and what kind of people lived them. I described what men endured, quoted what they wrote, and from this tried to trace what changed in their hearts. By doing so I hoped first to understand them, then to depict their lives and times, and what they left the future.

On style, Greek drama explains some of my quirks. For example, the book is written to be spoken aloud. You see this in frequent commas which serve didactic and dramatic purposes in slowing readers down, in readiness to begin sentences with 'And' or 'But' to keep momentum, in the use of alliteration, and in puns, as where I write of Pozieres that 'the merciless shells rained' (reigned) (163).

But other factors shaped my style more. Growing up in rural Australia encouraged economy of words. People like Eric Fry in the History Department encouraged clarity and simplicity, although I think I used too many adjectives and adverbs. I tried to follow Bean's example, which he maintained over more words than any other Australian, of never writing a word which could not be understood by a fourteen-year-old. Three words in the thesis, I think, failed Bean's example, and two remain in the book: 'maelstrom' (xvii) and 'miasma' (72). I could not think of simpler alternatives.

Stylistically my main aim is not to intrude into the story. Intrusion is there, of course, in every word, chosen or written, unavoidably. I mean that I tried not to make intrusion obvious, to let the story unfold as seemingly as it did at the time. Narrative is history's highest art. At least once I did not succeed, in discussing discipline (236–38). This is the weakest part of the book, not because of the topic or the conclusion, but because I shoulder aside those who matter and talk from centre stage. A sense of how things seemed at the time is broken.

A thesis depends on its sources. Mine inspired and shaped my thinking, and after all I did to them they remain its core and its most memorable quality. Never forget the primacy of sources. I have a poignant memory of their power. After the thesis was published as a book, in 1974, an old lady wrote from Adelaide about a letter a man wrote to his pregnant wife from the slaughter of Pozieres. The letter concluded:

> The place is like Hell darling but ... it is better to die for you and country than to be a cheat of the empire ... God be with you Love for all Time ... Remember me to baby when she is Born—if a boy don't make him a tin soldier but should war break out, let him enlist and do his bit if not he'll be no son of mine (168).

The man was killed soon after; the old lady was his wife. She had never heard of his letter until she saw the book, and she wrote to say that her son became a squadron leader in World War II, and that she was thankful to learn after so long that her husband would have approved, and what his parting thoughts were. That made it all worthwhile. But there was more to the story, which I did not tell her, or anyone. Sometimes life is too big for art.

A writer must *choose* a voice. You have many voices; it is never possible to be a mere conduit of your evidence. You are part of your work. Be conscious of this, choose a voice, work to develop it. Which voice you choose will depend on what you want to say. That will be informed by what your evidence directs, by what the times suggest, and by the art of combining these. Do not take lightly the tremendous opportunity a thesis gives you; make sure you say something worthwhile.

ENDNOTE

[1] B. Gammage, 'The Broken Years: A Study of the Diaries and Letters of Australian Soldiers in the Great War, 1914–18', PhD thesis, Australian National University, 1970. The thesis was later published as a book, *The Broken Years: Australian Soldiers in the Great War*, Australian National University Press, Canberra, 1974. References in the text are to the book.

CHAPTER 3

POSTMODERNITY AND THE RELEASE OF THE CREATIVE IMAGINATION

Donna Merwick

A rather curious and sobering thing happened to me as I was reading in preparation for this paper. I had expected to encounter a certain kind of literature in confronting the subject of postmodernity. It would be full of word games. There would be parodic essays on the supposed distinction between late modernity and postmodernity. There would be voices asserting or, alternatively, denying that ours is an age of all surface and no depth. Some would argue that it's a world of mobility rather than substance, of the fragment rather than the whole, or of heterogeneities rather than totalities. We live, others would agree, by cheap commodification rather than community-building. I anticipated the teasing word constructions that baffle the uninitiated: the double-coding, the 'aesthetic play'.[1] I was, as I say, prepared for this discourse. Over the years, I have in fact learned a great deal from it. I enjoy it. This time, however, something discordant struck me in some of the literature. Subtly evident was an expression of deep personal disturbance or anger not at all in keeping with the ordinary gamesmanship and paradox-play or, as often, the dense analysis characteristic of postmodern theorising. Let me give some examples.

Frank Ankersmit is a demanding writer. He is a Dutch philosopher of history. He publishes in a number of European journals and also in *History and Theory*, a journal set up at Wesleyan University for the studies of such scholars. In a 1989 article on 'Historiography and Postmodernism', Ankersmit set out to make an argument in defence of the practices of postmodern writing, especially history. His way of doing it was in sentences like these, one following the other: 'The point is that in an intentional context like this, p can never be replaced by another statement, even if the other statement is equivalent to p, or results directly from it.'[2] This was the expected taut analytic prose. It was properly impersonal and ran to sixteen pages! But suddenly Ankersmit yielded to what can only be termed an outburst of anger. Examining historicism, and its central feature of essentialism, he hit out at certain of its practitioners. Historicism had made its entry, he wrote pointedly, 'particularly in Germany'. He allowed himself to describe the historians of such a position. They were academics filled with an 'optimistic self-overestimation'. 'Anyone', he went on, 'cannot fail to notice the *ludicrous* nature of their pretensions'.[3] Ludicrous is not a word Ankersmit would ordinarily use—or be expected to use—in a work of analytic philosophy. It is an extreme characterisation, bordering on the unprofessional. Here we have, perhaps, a window let open for just a moment: a Dutch man's comment about Germany and a time in its recent history from which (he is at pains to show) postmodernity has to its credit declared itself separate and apart.

Consider one of Jean-François Lyotard's essays as well. It is not easy to convince students to read his influential and long essay, *The Postmodern Condition: A Report on Knowledge*. Perhaps it is enough to say that the essay (sometimes laboriously) relates postmodernism to the sociology of knowledge and describes our 'postmodern condition' as one of looking both back on and forward to modernism. For the most part, Lyotard, a Frenchman, stays within the stylistic parameters of an exposition given over to theoretical matters and the concise assemblage of data and interpretation. In a final impassioned paragraph, however, his work comes to resemble Ankersmit's. He turns to those thinkers—the icons of German philosophy of history, Kant and Hegel—who had tried to totalise into a 'unity' a social and metaphysical world that, he declares, any analysis will show is manifestly heterogeneous. The French writer chooses his words carefully here, immediately identifying German historicism as not even rational but as a concession to desire. It was a '*yearning* for totality'. And it related itself to nothing less than the coming of terror. Kant, Hegel, and implicitly their historicist followers, he writes, 'knew that the price to pay for such an illusion [as totality] is terror'. 'The nineteenth and twentieth centuries', he goes on, 'have given us as much terror as we can take. We have paid a high enough price for the nostalgia of the whole and [of] the one'. Can we now once again, Lyotard asks,

> hear the mutterings of the desire for a return to terror, for the realisation of the fantasy to seize the real. The answer is: Let us [in these times of postmodernity] wage war on totality … let us activate *the differences* and save the honor of the name.[4]

One could layer on this perspective—what I would for the moment want to call a European perspective—the writings of the French philosopher Emmanuel Levinas and the German theologian Hans Kung.[5] It is Walter Benjamin, however, who most strongly articulates 'the terror' that results from yearning for unities and totalities. Like Ankersmit and Lyotard, he gives a place in his writings to meanings that should, one would think, keep their proper place outside the margins of theoretical, high-level philosophical discourse. Benjamin was a German Jew, a philosopher who took his own life after failing to escape from Germany and the Gestapo. Tragically, he had already made the connection between a yearning for totality and terror. He situated each in Hitler's Nazi Germany. For more than anything else, fascism was able to legitimate itself by claiming to speak for a single national identity. And it had at hand a theory of the past to which many German academic historians were committed. Their historicism preached 'a unity and ... a continuity of history'. They wrote repeatedly of history as progress. The very passage of time was the advancement 'toward a betterment'—implicitly toward the Third Reich. But Benjamin argued that they were (at best) naïve in their understanding of history and power, for it is '*the victor* who forever represents the present conquest or the present victory as an improvement in relation to the past'. Real history, he wrote, is that of those 'traumatised by history'. It is the story of those 'oppressed by the new victory', even while the historians of the victor uncritically espouse 'his [and his regime's] narrative perspective'. History is the story of those who, amid the 'deafening' voices of the victors, are reduced to silence.[6]

For Benjamin, history is not a seamless narrative. It is always ruptured because it is always and only 'the transmission of historical discourse from ruler to ruler, from one historical instance of power to another'. With his own times in mind, he concludes in one of his essays that 'the continuum of history is that of the oppressors'. Continuity is 'a process of silencing'. 'The history of the oppressed is discontinuous.' Its purpose, moreover, is not truth but redemption.[7]

I've mentioned Benjamin's fellow European, Emmanuel Levinas. His ideas are parallel to Benjamin's. Writing as early as the 1960s but still being published in the 1990s, his work is also 'dominated by the presentiment and the memory of the Nazi horror'. He writes that what we have of the past are only traces of the past. Presences are there but absences too, simultaneously. Our task? 'The invisible must manifest itself if history is to lose its right to the last word, necessarily unjust ... inevitably cruel.'[8]

I wanted to put this set of analyses before you because I was startled, and moved, by the way trauma, terror and deep emotion had seeped into writings that were either directly or indirectly confronting the issues entailed in describing and evaluating postmodernity. I also wanted to use them as a counter-weight to the discourse of those who are antagonists to postmodernism and postmodernity. The words of such critics are marked by a derision that, in my experience, few other proponents of a discourse position have incited. I've wanted to say that, on the contrary, the realities for which the words postmodernism and postmodernity are, after all, only stand-ins are in some of their origins and in their present operations far from deserving of contempt.

But listen for a moment to what I mean by contemptuous. In a January 1999 issue of the *Times Literary Supplement*, Gertrude Himmelfarb reviewed a book by Professor

James W. Caesar, entitled *Reconstructing America: The Symbol of America in Modern Thought*. She began the review:

> It is perversely heartening to know that at least some of the follies and miseries that are so much with us today have been with us for centuries. If we have survived them so long, perhaps we can continue to bear with them.

It is also agreeable, she continued, 'to find that a scholar can be passionate in pursuit of his subject without in any way impairing his scholarship'. Such a scholar is Professor Caesar whose book opens, she went on, with a 'remarkable confession':

> If it were acceptable in a work of modern scholarship to rise with indignation in the defense of one's country, I would begin this book with a simple call to arms. It is time to take America back. It is time to take it back from the literary critics, philosophers and self-styled postmodern thinkers who have made the very name 'America' a symbol for that which is grotesque, obscene, monstrous, stultifying, stunted, levelling, deadening, deracinating, deforming, rootless, uncultured and—always in quotations marks—'free'.[9]

This is the sort of shrill and contemptuous dismissal of postmodernism with which, I think, we are all familiar. Australia, and Australian political discourse, is not free of it, not in its substance, not in its shrillness. However, we have been asked to think about postmodernity in relation to *positive* notions about the creative aspects of writing histories and writing cultures. We are here to consider our current cultural conditions and, if we can, discover in them positive challenges to perform our work—our research and writing—in new and exemplary ways. In this, we are perhaps led in the direction of John Frow, an Australian literary critic who insists that, define it or describe it as you like, postmodernity makes certain things possible.[10]

Perhaps I have been asked to consider these issues with you because I have said again and again—to students, colleagues and readers—that I would not want to be performing my work (in my case, writing history) at any time other than now. Surely postmodernity is a word invented to cover the sets of conditions within which we now live and that exert pressures on our aesthetic practices—as physicists and business managers, as scientists and architects and novelists. I take my obligation to understand that set of conditions very seriously. I do so because my writing is unavoidably a cultural artefact produced within them. I want it to count. So I need to know how cultural objects are produced in this time of postmodernity, how they are consumed and validated. Along with others (but not everyone), I believe very firmly that in the social, economic and cultural conditions of our times, of postmodernity, we of the west are and have been experiencing a paradigm shift. I'm not foolish enough to engage in—or to engage you in—debating the specifics of that shift: exactly when it could be noted and became operative in each discipline and each national economy, exactly why we are heterophiliac and not essentialists, why we have come to problematise the taken-for-granted practices and beliefs of yesteryear. There is an oblique way of expressing this. At the least, it has the advantage of not being contentious: postmodernity is a 'situation the interpretive conditions of which can no longer be described as modernity'.[11]

Let me stay with this notion of problematising, however, and look once again at Benjamin's work. This time I want to read it for the certainties he considers problematic. I discover that these are some of the certainties he brings under question: that the passage of time is the continuous advancement of reason; that the proper narratives relating this passage of time must be and can be scientific, that historical writing is apolitical, objective, driven by a search for truth or for the essence of a subject. He queries the assumption that history texts, claiming objectivity and truth-telling, are essentially neutral in relation to power. He also tests its claim that somehow it has successfully set itself apart from those genres where contaminants such as subjectivity, a concern for style, 'yearnings' and other non-rational impulses have a place.

The certainties that were untenable to Benjamin are untenable to me as well. For me, postmodernity—the culture that is ours today—provides a space for problematising those certainties. I know that such a space was not there when, for example, I was a graduate student at the University of Wisconsin in the mid 1960s. Or, if such a space was there, it was only as wide as a handful of scholars like Hayden White and Norman O. Brown (and, I suspect, Manning Clark in Australia) were pushing at it to be.[12] In the process of problematising my discipline and its certainties and in making my own determinations about the boundaries I want to set to that enterprise, I have experienced a release of the imagination and a challenge to perform as a writer that I would not have thought possible.[13] It is not that I have discovered problems ignored within the tradition of historical writing. But what one is doing is finding 'ways of speaking' that make 'old ways of speaking optional'.[14] For, like the German historicists, I have also read the evidence of the past. I too have encountered it in archives. I have watched myself work as a researcher and as a writer, and I have observed my colleagues and students at their work. It is not the case that truth is there in the archives waiting to be discovered; it is not the case that finding the truth is the sole or necessarily the highest purpose of history-writing. It is not the case that the historian is practising some kind of positivistic science. Rather, it is an art form—or if it is a mix of the two, art and science, then let us accept this as our challenge and illumination.

We are in the business of constructing representations. The subject of representation has often been debated and theorised and, at such times, a space has invariably been opened for the new, for experimentation. One thinks of the Renaissance, or of Haarlem or Rome in the mid seventeenth century. Ours, I think, stands alongside those times, debating, theorising, puzzling over the copy and the original, arguing about the fit between the text and the image, daring the new. For some commentators today, representations will always be impaired because they are just appearances. They are not the real thing and, worse yet, their makers don't even claim them to be. No claim is made for authenticity.[15] The movie of *The Client*, the book *The Client*: which of these is authentic, which is a copy of which, or doesn't anyone care? Many others equate the copy with the superficial. After all, we live every day with films and fashion designs that are marketed as the thing to see or to buy *because* they are simply simulations of the original. We live on the surface, it is said. We and those who are the custodians of our culture lack depth. Against this, others will ask whether 'depth' is not itself a metaphor, a western European construct and therefore not necessarily privileged over surface. Moreover, can we ever do anything more than interpret 'the effects of the real'?[16]

Within these wide-open queries and discourses, we make our representations. We offer our performances. If we have the courage, we put on the market our experiments. I'm not suggesting that everything is up for grabs; I'm not suggesting that everything should be, for whatever reason, unsettled. I am arguing that any performance today, any exercise of the creative imagination in the cause of presenting knowledge, must be made with the fullest possible understanding of the intellectual atmosphere within which it is put forward for examination and acceptance. This is not to say that we need to get an understanding of postmodernity because it is *the cause* of what we are performing. Cultural artefacts or performances, as we know, are not determined by a regnant socio-economic base or set of political structures. The conditions called 'postmodernity' have an influence but cultural performances have their own rules. And this is true for poetry and legal narratives, for scientific papers and architectural drawings. Perhaps it is best to cast this in terms of performance and audience.[17] The audience out there, the community out there, will or will not legitimate our work. Neither the sciences nor the arts can legitimate themselves.[18]

To be consistent, I think I should perform something of mine for you. Its title is *Death of a Notary: Conquest and Change in Colonial New York*.[19] This is the Preface or, as I called it, 'Epitaph':

> He was the only one. He was the only man to have committed suicide in the town's seventeenth-century history.
>
> I first met him when I was writing another book on Albany, New York. He was the town notary. In a way he stood in the background, bearing witness to the contracts, promises and pledges of other townspeople. His occupation put him somewhere within the Dutch legal system. I, however, have always thought of him as being someone like myself, a historian. He was surrounded by stories, those he listened to and recorded, the hundreds he archived in a chest or trunk where they receded into the past.
>
> Adriaen Janse van Ilpendam hanged himself on March 12, 1686. I wish I knew how it happened. This is not because of prurience, I think, but because I hope there was some comfort in the moment of his death, that it was not too terrible. Only one man that I know of, an early twentieth-century archivist, has puzzled over Janse's suicide. He guessed that it was related to the English conquest of Janse's home, New Netherland. Since he earned his livelihood by writing legal papers in Dutch, the demand that they be written in English moved him to his tragic decision.
>
> The archivist was, I believe, correct. And perhaps he was right too in leaving the matter at that. I am still puzzled, however, at how it was that an imperial power's designs for territorial acquisition, military invasion and occupation, visions of continental hegemony, how those forces met with and made a casualty of so small a life as Janse's. England's grand designs did not include his death. He was so incidental.
>
> Janse's life, which you will read about, was not a prelude to his suicide. Only later readers of his life would see it that way. It was a sequence of experiences. That, at least, is what we have to think after reading

the records. And I have presented them for you in that way. Like his suicide, they are also mysterious happenings in a culture that is not ours, each a meetingplace of circumstance and structure, of particularities and generalities. Some were under his control; most were not. We can only ever know some of them. Puzzling over his experiences, I have come to think that no society, neither New Netherland before the English invasion of 1664 nor New York after it, makes it easy for someone to get along. Getting along in the New World in the seventeenth century was immensely difficult. Perhaps the difficulties were great enough to let us think that some people, some colonists like Adriaen Janse, would have been better off had they never come.

As we begin, I owe Adriaen Janse an apology. He never referred to himself as Adriaen Janse or Adriaen Janse van Ilpendam. He always wrote Adriaen van Ilpendam. You will see why. How he would otherwise tell a different story of himself from the one I tell, I don't know. I do know that, like me, he would pull it together from fragments. He would draw on bits of memory, records, perhaps the oft-repeated anecdotes of others. He would shape it to suit his audience. Some facts or memories he would call upon if he were testifying in court. Others were good for yarning with friends. His selection would satisfy the occasion. I hope that in telling Janse's story, I have judged the occasion of your reading about him correctly.

We are told that in any military adventure, the first casualty is truth. I think it is not. Janse is a reminder that the first casualties are people.

I wrote those words, just seven paragraphs. And I like what they are and what they do. But in reading them, I know that in a sense they are not just my words. They are there because I have received the gift of being able to write in *these times*—these times, if you will, of postmodernity. From somewhere, from some set of interpretive conditions, some background, surely from reading the performances of others and being the beneficiary of their creative imagination, I thought that, among other things, I could legitimately be a story-teller. I could find a voice for speaking to readers. I could disregard history as a medium offering information and, instead, do as a story-teller does, that is, embed the experiences of Adriaen Janse in my own life and thinking in order to 'pass it on *as experience* to those listening'.[20]

I tried to write with honest respect for my readers. I tried, for example, to meet their ability to discern that a story written of Janse's life would necessarily be constructed, that if the story were in his own hands it would be none the less constructed. His story would be like the narrative of an academic historian lecturing to students or that of a mother talking to a young child: it would fit a context and take a shape from it. Readers are not at all unsettled by a writer who is saying that there is no single or true perspective on a subject. Simply: there is Adriaen Janse in people's memories, in court records, in anecdotes, in my story, in the stories of him that readers will themselves construct as they read along in the book. Such pluralism is acceptable today because it meets, as it seems to me, 'our social and metaphysical reality'.[21] I don't think, in short, that undecidability disturbs readers.

We can, I think, credit readers with another kind of reading skill. Adriaen Janse was really the smallest of figures on any world scene. Yet the insignificance of his life reveals universal problems and meanings. This supposed insignificance needs to be addressed. As Nietzsche put it, in good history-writing 'the simple is lost in the profound, and the profound in the simple'.[22] Readers can catch the paradox of that as well. Forgive me if this begins to seem a bit patronising in regard to readers. The fact is we need legitimation for our questions, our research and our interpretations. The community gives this. It is readers who 'bring … [this legitimacy] to meet the writer'.[23]

In *Death of a Notary*, I did not introduce theory or theoretical considerations. But who can think of words and narratives taking their shape from contexts without thinking of Ludwig Wittgenstein and John Austin? Who can read the phrase, 'his experiences … are also mysterious happenings in a culture that is not ours', without simultaneously bringing to mind the cross-cultural studies of James Clifford and Clifford Geertz, Greg Dening and Marshall Sahlins, Homi Bhabha. Who can think of the constructed nature of the past without recalling the work of Michel Foucault, or think of history as an art form without conjuring the names of Hayden White and Arthur Danto, Michel de Certeau and Roland Barthes.

We need to be careful when speaking of postmodernity. We need to avoid the error that the great early twentieth-century scientist Alfred North Whitehead identified as 'misplaced concreteness'. The conditions of our culture are continually changing. As much as postmodernity, processes such as globalisation, cosmopolitanism and hybridisation are much discussed now and will affect the way we perform our work. The aesthetic—or call it our cultural production—is always integrated into economic production. We don't know, however, how the conditions of that relationship will change.[24] The kind of knowledge that a future audience may construe as necessary may well be very different from that which satisfied the 1990s. It will still, however, be the task of creative imagination to discover what, in our own work, can ethically and responsibly meet that need.

ENDNOTES

1.   F. Jameson, 'Foreword', in J. Lyotard, *The Postmodern Condition: A Report on Knowledge*, trans. G. Bennington and B. Massumi, University of Minnesota Press, Minneapolis, 1984, p. xviii.

2.   F.R. Ankersmit, 'Historiography and Postmodernism', *History and Theory: Studies in the Philosophy of History*, vol. 28, no. 2, 1989, p. 144.

3.   *Ibid.*, pp. 148–49, my emphasis.

4.   Lyotard, *Postmodern Condition*, pp. 81–82, my emphasis.

5.   For Levinas, see R. Eaglestone, 'The "Fine Risk" of History: Post-Structuralism, the Past, and the Work of Emmanuel Levinas', *Rethinking History*, vol. 2, no. 3, 1998, pp. 313–20. Hans Kung accepts the validity of the term postmodernity, identifying modernity as Euro-centric, marked by a defunct belief in reason and progress, and enunciated within 'a narrow nationalistic framework'. *A Global Ethic for a Global Politics and Economics*, trans. J. Bowden, Oxford University Press, New York, 1998, p. 67.

6.   S. Felman, 'Benjamin's Silence', *Critical Inquiry*, vol. 25, no. 2, 1999, pp. 209–10, my emphasis.

7.   *Ibid.*, p. 210, quoting W. Benjamin, *Paralipomènes et variantes des Thèses* 'Sur le concept de l'histoire', in J. Monnoyer (ed.), *Ecrits Français*, Gallimard, Paris, 1991, p. 352.

8.   Eaglestone, 'The "Fine Risk" of History,' p. 317, quoting Levinas, *Difficult Freedom*, trans. Saen Hand, Athlone, London, 1990, pp. 219, 319. Levinas's main critique of totalities is in this statement: '*Our responsibility for the other* … interrupts totalising Western all-consuming reason', p. 315, my emphasis.

9.   G. Himmelfarb, 'Review of James W. Caesar, *Reconstructing America: The Symbol of America in Modern Thought* (Yale University Press, New Haven, 1997)', *Times Literary Supplement*, no. 4996, 1999, p. 5.

10.   J. Frow, *Time and Commodity Culture: Essays in Cultural Theory and Postmodernity*, Clarendon Press, Oxford, 1997, p. 4.

11.   C. Jencks, *What Is Postmodernism?*, Academy Editions, London, 1986, p. 35, quoting R. Krauss, 'Sculpture in the Expanded Field', in H. Foster (ed.), *The Anti-Aesthetic: Essays on Postmodern Culture*, Port Townsend, Washington, 1983, p. 39. For one of many comment-

ators who accept the notion of a paradigm shift, see P. Portoghesi, quoted in L. Hutcheon, *A Poetics for Postmodernism: History, Theory, Fiction*, Routledge, New York, 1988, p. 22.

12 I have in mind N.O. Brown, *Life Against Death: The Psychoanalytical Meaning of History*, Wesleyan University Press, Middletown, Conn., 1959, and *Love's Body*, Random House, New York, 1966, but particularly H.V. White, 'The Burden of History', *History and Theory*, vol. 5, no. 2, 1966, pp. 111–34. This essay held the seeds of his magisterial work, *Metahistory: The Historical Imagination in Nineteenth-Century Europe*, Johns Hopkins University Press, Baltimore, 1973. Ankersmit calls this book 'the most revolutionary book in philosophy of history over the past twenty-five years', 'Historiography', p. 143.

13 Throughout *A Poetics for Postmodernism*, Hutcheon addresses the matter of problematising traditional certainties in disciplines such as history.

14 Hutcheon, *A Poetics for Postmodernism*, p. 14, quoting R. Rorty, 'Deconstruction and Circumvention', *Critical Inquiry*, vol. 11, no. 1, 1984, pp. 1–23.

15 See, for example, T. Brennan, *At Home in the World: Cosmopolitanism Now*, Harvard University Press, Cambridge, Mass., 1997.

16 Frow, *Time and Commodity Culture*, p. 11.

17 Jencks, in *What Is Postmodernism?*, points out that the impulse to reach out for a wider audience is itself a feature of postmodernity, p. 7

18 Ankersmit, 'Historiography', pp. 146–47, and see Jenks, *What is Postmodernism?*, p. 22.

19 Cornell University Press, Ithaca, 1999.

20 Benjamin, 'On Some Motifs in Baudelaire', in his *Illuminations: Essays and Reflections*, Harcourt, Brace & World, New York, 1969, p. 159, cited Felman, 'Benjamin's Silence', p. 226, my emphasis.

21 Jencks, *What Is Postmodernism?*, p. 22.

22 F. Nietzsche, *The Use and Abuse of History*, in *Thoughts Out of Season*, 5, Works, Russell & Russell, New York, 1964, p. 55.

23 Ankersmit, 'Historiography', p. 147, quoting J. Huizinga, *De Taak der Cultuurgeschiedenis* in J. Huizinga, *Verzamelde Werken*, vol. 7, H.D. Tjeenk, Haarlem, 1950, p. 72.

24 Frow, *Time and Commodity Culture*, p. 1.

CHAPTER 4

WRITING FROM FRAGMENTS

John Docker

> What the historians called a 'fragment' — a weaver's diary, a collection
> of poems by an unknown poet (and to these we might add all those
> literatures of India that Macaulay condemned, creation myths and
> women's songs, family genealogies, and local traditions of history) — is
> of central importance in … thinking other histories.[1]

It's rare to know how a book is written. A book catches our eye in a favourite bookshop; we think we must buy it, forget the price; before idling towards the cash register, we might look at what's said on the back cover, the information on the inside jacket, the photograph (if any) of the author, perhaps the index to see what family of names is being invoked and discussed. We might quickly glance at the preface and acknowledgements, which tell some of the story of how the book came to be, but not usually all that much, or not enough. How is the book first thought? How does it proceed from a mere gleam in its creator's eye? How does it go from a vague idea involving obscure desires and passions, fantasies and obsessions, to the first shape of an argument, a thesis with a thesis, a narrative where chapters start to relate to each other and that begins to move as if of itself, as if naturally? What I'd like to do in this essay is try to recall the process of getting going, the first moves I made, while recognising that memory is unreliable and always constructing; what memory creates becomes another story. What I seek to do is remember the messiness, how haphazard it was, the luck involved, the clues picked up in conversations over coffee or hearing a seminar or conference paper.

Often, I think, the effect of an unfolding narrative is a very late happening in the whole process, perhaps occurring in the final revising (though that can be a long period). Certainly, in my case, that's what I found when I was writing, for most of the 1990s, my book, *1492: The Poetics of Diaspora* (published in 2000 by Continuum). One thing I knew: I wanted this new book to be very different in spirit and temper from my previous book, *Postmodernism and Popular Culture: A Cultural History*. I wanted the two books to be in tension, to possess almost a contradictory relationship.

My *Postmodernism and Popular Culture* came out in 1994, a generally positive evocation of the continuities between carnival and carnivalesque in early modern Europe and twentieth-century popular culture, building on theories of comedy and of language and textuality generally that I very much admire, those of Mikhail Bakhtin, especially in *Rabelais and His World*. While I was completing *Postmodernism and Popular Culture*, my mind—materially aided by the award in 1993 of a five-year Australian Research Council fellowship to research ethnic and cultural identities—was already turning to another 'life' interest. I wished to address the challenging productive debates that had been coursing for over a decade, in many ways inspired by Edward W. Said's *Orientalism* (1978), that addressed issues of colonialism, postcolonialism, migration, diaspora, exile, belonging, identity, ethnicity and 'race'. I was interested in these debates for autobiographical as well as intellectual reasons; indeed, I could see no distinction between the autobiographical and the intellectual, ideas and being. I felt I could apply my 'cultural history' approach to these issues, an approach I had explored in *Postmodernism and Popular Culture* as well as in my previous writing: the approach of someone trained in literary studies yet who wishes to sustain conversations between literary theory and other fields, not least cultural theory, the history of ideas, intellectual history, political history and historiography.

In the final writing of *Postmodernism and Popular Culture*, I brought some of these interests to bear on Bakhtin. I observed that Bakhtin's theory of carnival in early modernity lacked a sense of Europe's others, that it didn't hear Caliban's wounded voice, that Bakhtin's critical imagination was landlocked: colonial expansion by Europe during the Renaissance and later seems not to have attracted his theoretical curiosity. While *Rabelais and His World* insists on heterogeneity, awareness of the other, and self-criticality, I suggested that it nevertheless plays down the presence and consequences of European ethnocentrism. In this connection I noted how carnival and its associated activities could produce hostility to, demonising of, violence towards, foreigners or those conceived as outsiders: to ethnic and religious minorities like Jews and Turks, to witches, prostitutes, actors, even to animals like cocks, dogs, cats, and pigs. The Roman carnival included a race for Jews, offering a sadistic opportunity for throwing mud and stones at them as they passed.

I began to feel that when the book-to-be finally developed its own voice and rhythm, it would probably be a kind of dark sequel to *Rabelais and His World* and *Postmodernism and Popular Culture*.

By 'poetics' in the title of *1492: The Poetics of Diaspora* I intended to suggest that we necessarily understand or try to understand identity and belonging, or not belonging, through cultural forms—through representation as in genre, myth, novel, poem, allegory, parable, anecdote, story, sayings, metaphors, puns and riddles. By 'poetics' I also had something else obscurely, secretly, in mind: I wanted to return to writing about literary texts, even 'high' literary texts. I wanted to move away from a certain emphasis in Cultural Studies I thought was in danger of locking itself in as a convention or orthodoxy: that 'we' in Cultural Studies don't do literary analysis, or at least we don't do close literary analysis of texts like literary critics do. Yet it would seem to be obvious that many of those who practise literary studies have for a long time now gone way beyond the restrictive formalism and attention only to canonical texts of 'high literature', associated in the twentieth century with New Criticism. Such surely is obvious from movements like New Historicism or in postcolonial literary studies. Furthermore, one activity of Cultural Studies has been the close analysis of diverse kinds of semiotic and cultural material. When I contemplated returning to close analysis of literary texts, including 'high' texts, in *1492* it was with joyful, fearful, anticipation.

I felt the best place to start would be a detailed re-reading of Joyce's *Ulysses*. I knew from early on that I would like to stage a contrast between the portrait in *Ulysses* of Leopold Bloom, the most famous evocation of a Jewish character in modern literature, and the portrait of Mordecai Himmelfarb in Patrick White's *Riders in the Chariot* (1961); I'd been interested in *Riders in the Chariot* for a long time, since I'd talked about it in different terms in my *Australian Cultural Elites* (1974), and now I wanted to come back to the ways it constructed ethnicity, in particular Jewishness in Himmelfarb. Analysing *Ulysses* also led quickly to Salman Rushdie's *The Satanic Verses*, especially the similarity of heretical porkeating near the beginning of both novels. I had decided that *The Satanic Verses* was the great postmodern novel, and the successor to *Ulysses* as the great modernist novel, soon after it controversially came out in 1988. Then at a conference on cross-cultural literatures in the mid 1990s I heard a paper by a visiting Indian scholar which talked of the Jewish characters in Rushdie's *The Moor's Last Sigh*. I bought the novel the next morning, and immediately began to read into it. What particularly struck me was the story framing the novel, relating contemporary India to the fall of the last of Moorish Spain in Granada in 1492.

'1492'—as a series of connected events and as a kind of iconic and mythological moment in literary and cultural history, perhaps in European and Western and world history—began to intrigue me. I began to read as much as I could about '1492', to learn that three key happenings occurred within a very short time near the beginning of that fateful year: Columbus sailed for the Americas; eight centuries of Moorish Spain finally ended in the surrender by the sultan Boabdil of Granada, with its legendary fortress-palace the Alhambra; and the Jews of Spain, except for those who in perilous circumstances had chosen or had been forced to convert to Catholicism (becoming known as *conversos*), were subject to one of history's recurring crimes against humanity, mass expulsion.

Then by one of those pieces of luck, someone—I must have been talking to a fellow literary critic—said, 'Why don't you also look at Walter Scott's *Ivanhoe*, it mentions Moorish Spain and Boabdil's Granada'. And indeed it does. At novel's end Rebecca, the black-tressed dark-eyed daughter of Isaac of York, has a famous conversation with the 'fair Rowena', now married to Wilfred of Ivanhoe. Rebecca tells the surprised Saxon princess that she and her father will leave England: 'I leave it, lady, ere this moon again changes. My father hath a brother high in favour with Mohammed Boabdil, King of Grenada—thither we go, secure of peace and protection, for the payment of such ransom as the Moslem exact from our people.' Rebecca and Isaac will somehow have to travel from late twelfth-century England, when the novel is set, to late fifteenth-century Spain.

Much later, indeed in the final revising year of 1999, I realised that '1492' provided the frame-story not only for *Ivanhoe* and *The Moor's Last Sigh*, but for Amin Maalouf's 1986 *Leo the African* and Richard Zimler's 1998 *The Last Kabbalist of Lisbon*. By 'realised' I should say that a visiting scholar to the Centre for Cross-Cultural Research at the ANU suggested over coffee that I should read Maalouf's novel, which he thought very highly of.[2] And Ann Curthoys, in our favourite Sydney bookshop, Gleebooks, espied near the front of the store's new novels *The Last Kabbalist of Lisbon*, drawing it to my grateful attention. With the help of friends, new acquaintances and loved ones—amused observers of an obvious obsessive—I was building up a body of '1492' literary texts, a working archive.

'1492' as an idea, rich in literary and historical implications, a meeting point for diverse world cultural histories and religions, was starting to suggest itself as the frame-story of my book-in-process. It struck me that '1492' was a disaster not only for the Caribbean and the Americas but for Europe itself, because it enforced a notion of the emergent modern nation-state as ideally unified in ethnicity, religion, culture and mores. Such a notion became an assumption, and frequently led to the further notion that the nation-state should be based on ethnic superiority, separateness, and contempt or hatred for other nation-states. '1492' established in Christian Europe the authority of notions of blood purity and blood lines in the defining of who was a true citizen, who truly belonged in a society: in Iberia the Statutes of the Purity of Blood were used to discriminate against New Christians (former Moors and Jews who had become *conversos*), while favouring Old Christians. The New Christians became internal enemies to be surveilled, disciplined, punished by the Inquisition on behalf of the rest of the population; they were to be spied on and reported to the state authorities by neighbours, by people one regarded as one's friends, by family. '1492' created the European and Western nation-state as a metaphysics of desire: to be truly human, truly civilised, people had to live in a strong and organised nation-state; those peoples who don't have a strong state and unified nation are lesser in the scale of humanity and perhaps less than human. Those from within and without who threaten the ideal unity of the post-1492 nation-state are to be regarded as the foreigner, the stranger, the outsider. Such a metaphysics with its associated tests of proper blood and proper bodies and proper descent led to the catastrophe of nineteenth-century European racism and its culmination, Nazism and the Holocaust. The desire to create internal and external enemies, a desire descending from the Inquisition, led to the disaster of the Cold War and to a grotesque society of surveillance like East Germany with its Stasi. Every apparently democratic egalitarian society in Europe and the West and the world influenced and shaped by Europe and the West remains in danger from the resurgence of such notions and conceptions.

I began to appreciate how much '1492' signified a double movement in early modern and modern history: the development of a desire for a unified culture and strong nation-state within Europe, accompanied by imperial and colonial expansion. '1492' as an idea and series of events linked Europe and the rest of the world which Europe wished to subdue. I became interested in the argument put forward by Ella Shohat, an Iraqi-Israeli-American cultural critic, that the implications of '1492' for Europe and the Americas are closely entwined. The reconquest by Christian forces of Muslim territories within Spain coincided with the *Conquista*, the invasion of the New World. In the Americas the *conquistadors* were the direct heirs to the *Reconquista* in Spain. The constant campaigns within Spain over a number of centuries against Muslims and Jews, as well as against heretics and witches, provided a repertoire of gendered racial discourse which could be immediately applied in the Americas, in the developing Spanish and Iberian Empires. The conceptual and disciplinary apparatus that was turned against Europe's immediate or internal others, in the Crusades and the Inquisition, was projected outward against Europe's distant or external others. Just as the Muslims and Jews were demonised and diabolised as drinkers of blood, cannibals, sorcerers, devils, savages, so too were the indigenous Americans and the Black Africans. The practices of the Inquisition, where Muslims and Jews were either killed, expelled, or forced to convert, were extended to the New World.[3] (However, I quickly decided I wouldn't pursue the American journey of '1492': there was an abundance of chroniclers and interpreters of the post-Columbian devastation of the ancient peoples, cultures and civilisations of the Caribbean and Americas.)

I was beginning to conceive a secret, smouldering hatred of Christian Europe as an accursed continent. Even the activities of carnival were influenced and shaped by such '1492' racial discourse; the poetics of carnival and carnivalesque that I once so admired now felt like ashes in the mouth. This smouldering hatred was accompanied by a desire to be interested in the value of other world histories, before 1492. I quickly realised from reading and research that the post-1492 notion of a unified nation-state is not necessary or even common in Middle Eastern and European history; the Hellenistic and Roman and Arab and Ottoman Empires had all been pluralistic, with a central power permitting a variety of communities, ethnic and religious, to co-exist: I have also become a perverse admirer of empires for being supra-national, cosmopolitan entities. Such co-existing, such *convivencia*, had been what in many ways Moorish Spain was famous for: from 712 to the fall of Granada in January 1492, Muslim and Christian and Jewish communities lived side by side in the Iberian peninsula, clutched in a long, intimate embrace, sharing a land, learning from one another, creating a remarkable period of literary and cultural and philosophical and scientific ferment and achievement, trading, intermarrying, misunderstanding, squabbling, competing, fighting: an historical scene diverse, boisterous, crowded with life, in a pattern of peoples already palimpsestial, the Arab and Berber Moors overlaying a society of Hispano-Romans, Basques, Visigoths, Jews; until in the *Reconquista* the triumphal Christians enforced a future that attempted a project no less violent for being impossible, forcing the Many into the One.[4]

I also quickly realised that there was a developing contemporary literature, in novels and critical analysis, in spirit apocalyptic and millennial, that yearned to reach back and evoke and recall the alternative and inspiring value of pre-1492 worlds where the destructive European nationalist desire for ethnic and cultural unity was not normative and defining. Through a review in the *London Review of Books* by cultural anthropologist James Clifford,[5] I learnt of a book I now treasure, Ammiel Alcalay's *After Jews and Arabs: Remaking Levantine Culture*, which describes a Levantine world characterised by cultural mixing, relative freedom of travel, and multilingualism. Alcalay suggests that the notion of the Jew as always pariah, outsider and wanderer, is a Eurocentric conception. For more than a thousand years of history in the Middle East, North Africa and Muslim Spain, Jews, like Christians, protected Peoples of the Book, did not live in ghettos, shared their lives with their Arab neighbours in intimate intricate ways, enjoyed religious and cultural autonomy, and prospered in multiple occupations. In Alcalay's view, the historic world of Islam established an internationalisation of space, a world of mobility, autonomy, diversity, translatability and fluidity, and yet was characterised by deep attachment to particular cities—a poetics of heterogeneity. Reading Alcalay led me to S.D. Goitein's great multi-volume work, *A Mediterranean Society*, a portrait of Jewish communities in the Arab world that draws on the Cairo *geniza*, the medieval collection of diverse documents in the synagogue storehouse in Fustat in Old Cairo—a synagogue much used by Jewish traders to India.[6]

In his essay in the *London Review of Books*, James Clifford mentioned Alcalay's *After Jews and Arabs* in passing, though it was enough for me to seek it immediately through Gleebooks; the writing of my book could not have been remotely possible if an excellent, helpful, clever worldly bookshop like Gleebooks didn't exist. Clifford was actually reviewing *In an Antique Land*, a fascinating novel by Amitav Ghosh, which attempts to find out, from tiny fragments in the Cairo *geniza* documents scattered since the 1890s in libraries around the world, about a twelfth-century slave called Bomma, who worked for a Jewish trader Abraham Ben Yiju living in India. Bomma, it appeared, went on long trading voyages back to Egypt and the Middle East on behalf of Ben Yiju (who preferred to stay in India) and also on behalf of himself as a merchant in his own right. The Indian narrator of *In an Antique Land* feels that the past presence of Bomma should give him 'a right to be there' in Egypt, 'a sense of entitlement' to belong to a remarkable Judeo-Islamic trading, social and cultural world that stretched from pre-1492 Moorish Spain and Morocco and Tunisia in the west, through the Levant and East Africa to India and China in the east. He also painfully realises that the predatory Portuguese in the late 1490s and early 1500s had cut India off from this Middle Eastern world, so that Indians and peoples of the Levant no longer recognised that they had once belonged to a shared space and time. Because of European colonialism both India and the Middle East had historically become more constricted, more confined. His utopian desire to recover this shared history, to imagine it as 'in some tiny measure, still retrievable', is shadowed by the dystopian fear that it has been lost to him forever. Yet the narrator still desires, in mourning and sorrow, to belong to that past international cosmopolitan world, to imagine himself back into it, to keep romancing the past characters and figures he has created in his narrative.[7]

I now realised that I too shared that utopian longing to romance, to recover in imagination and desire a sense of entitlement to belong to a pre-1492 Judeo-Islamic trading, social and cultural world that stretched from Moorish Spain through the Mediterranean to India and China. My book would represent my various attempts to gain that feeling of entitlement. But how? Ghosh could point to Bomma, the twelfth-century slave. I could point to nothing even remotely substantial. I quickly sensed that my utopian quest would be attended not only by dystopian fear of failure, the pathos of irrecoverability and distance, but also by comedy and farce. As utopian quester I would be a *shlemiel*, forever reminding myself as I wrote and constructed various arguments of my quest's absurdity and delusiveness; I would have to have an ever-present sense of self-parody, of rigorous self-mockery. My book would have to be a record of various attempts to seek a sense of entitlement, which I knew would be illusory whatever I did, to that pre-1492 world.

Instead of the assured past existence of a figure like Bomma in *In an Antique Land*, I sought an elusive entitlement through the romance of an absurd tattoo, the inscription of a figure I imagined as the *veiled stranger*, who might signify a long, long ago Moorish Spanish or Biblical ancestor. To the story of the tattoo I added an evocation of my favourite cuisines, in particular of journeying every night as I cooked into recipes that stretched from Moroccan and Middle Eastern and Mediterranean (medieval and contemporary) to Indian and South-east Asian foods. I wanted my book to have body, taste, smell, however ridiculous and illusory as a claim to entitlement. Thinking around and about these twin fantasies, on the skin and by ingestion, became the first chapter of the book.[8] After a false start at an introduction, where I had too much deferred to conventional 'postcolonial theory', I decided not to have an introduction at all, but to plunge straight into the book's narrative.

I could see my book obscurely imitating Homer's *Odyssey* and Joyce's *Ulysses*. It would offer a kind of mock-Odyssean journey into literature, memory, political history, that related to various fragments of my, as it were, mongrel diaspora ancestry, English, Jewish, Irish, Australian. It would take in certain Indian novels, because there it was following the wide sweep, the remarkable arc, of the pre-1492 Judeo-Islamic-Indian world I wanted to connect to. In terms of romancing Moorish Spain, I thought of a particular fragment of ancestry, through my mother. I recalled family stories she would tell that her English family, from the East End of London, was descended from Portuguese Jews. I knew now that many Spanish Jews came to Portugal after the decree of expulsion from Spain that was announced in 1492, and these were the Sephardi Jews. I conceived a fantasy, that my lineage through my mother could be traced back somehow from England to Holland to Portugal to Moorish Spain; and to further that fantasy I decided to hire a genealogist, actually my mother-in-law, to try and do a genealogical search. So far it appears from her painstaking and imaginative detective work that my ancestry is solidly Ashkenazi not Sephardi.

I was worried that a general reader not familiar with Jewish history would not know much at all about the distinction between the northern European Ashkenazim and the Jews of Spain, the Sephardim, who became a new diaspora after the 1492 expulsion. I was pleased that when I asked my genealogist to write in *1492* about my asking her to do the genealogy, she wrote that 'the only Ashkenazi I had ever heard of was Vladimir Ashkenazi the famous pianist'. She had 'never heard the word Sephardi', though, she added, she suspected I wanted my Dutch ancestors, if there were any, to be Sephardi. She says to herself: 'Sephardi or Ashkenazi? Facts are facts and I will follow where the genealogical path takes me.' I liked the slight sceptical quizzical note here, the suggestion of her strange son-in-law's obsessions. As author I also liked my genealogist speaking in a way that might connect with readers unfamiliar with these terms and histories. I wanted to give readers the experience of learning about the Sephardim, recalling my own experience not that long before, when, on buying in England Jane S. Gerber's *The Jews of Spain: A History of the Sephardic Experience* (1992), I read it, in fits of wakefulness, on the long flight from London to Sydney (or read quite a bit of it).[9] A great deal of scholarship is looking as though one always knew something, one was always at ease with some area of learning: I wanted to try and undo that scholarly play.

Another problem: How was I going to analyse the novels I wished to analyse as part of my journey? My test case here was Scott's *Ivanhoe*. I wanted to place early on in the book a substantial exploration of *Ivanhoe*, a novel that was remarkably popular around the world from the moment of its publication in 1819; but I didn't want to do such exploring in a conventional literary critical way, enclosed in a text narrowly conceived, and confining the novel to English literary and cultural history. Here I was immensely assisted in terms of method by Walter Benjamin's prologue to his *The Origin of German Tragic Drama* (and by my son Ned Curthoys having told me to read this great book). Benjamin writes that the artist shares with the philosopher the task of the representation of ideas, where representation proceeds by digression, an interrupted structure. Representation as digression, as interruption, will work through the unique and the extreme; representation seeks that which is exemplary, even if this exemplary character can be admitted only in respect of the merest fragment. Representation searches for the most singular and eccentric of phenomena; the representation of an idea cannot be considered successful unless the whole range of possible extremes it contains has been virtually explored.[10]

In *Ivanhoe*, intense, wonderfully melodramatic, cinematic, fantastical, I wished to evoke how different world histories in the late twelfth century meet and interact and conflict in the novel's jousting conversations—of English history involving competing Saxons and Normans, of the Crusaders returning Orientalised from the Orient they had wished to obliterate, of Jews as hoping to belong to the English society which despised and persecuted them as well as knowing they indeed belonged to the Judeo-Islamic medieval world, Mediterranean and beyond. In discussing the novel, and indeed in romancing Rebecca (such I could wryly observe myself doing)—created in the text in her 'contemplative melancholy' as learned, intelligent, noble, dignified, gentle, firm, commanding, just, tolerant, generous, and liberal in her faith and sympathies—I lighted on tiny details, the merest fragments: of the delicate food and refreshments partaken by Rebecca and Isaac, of her clothes, and her manner and conversation indicating her urbanity, education, knowledge of languages and medical skills. I then related such details to aspects of the Levantine Judeo-Arab scenography evoked by Alcalay in *After Jews and Arabs* and Goitein in *A Mediterranean Society*, including the remarkably sophisticated medieval Arab and Moorish Spanish cuisine, especially the importance of spices and the adventurous mixing of meats with fruits (indicating the widespread influence of the Persian ur-cuisine).[11]

The references in *Ivanhoe* to Rebecca's father Isaac trading in choice silks, myrrh and aloes, gold and silver work, suggest that Isaac and Rebecca can be imagined as being part of the Mediterranean trade with India: Goitein observes that over half of the commodities traded on the Mediterranean market were imported from India and the Far East. I also relate the portrait of Rebecca to Goitein's evocation of women's lives within medieval Judeo-Islamic society, especially their high standing and economic independence and variety of occupations and professions, their ease of travel, their favoured dress materials and colours, and their learning. I then fancifully relate Rebecca to certain notions of female divine power in Kabbalism, the mystical movement that began in twelfth-century Provence and spread to nearby Jewish communities in Spain.

Said, contemplating Romantic literature, has observed that we should take note of the 'sheer folly and derangement stirred up by the Orient in Europe'.[12] By the end of my analysis of *Ivanhoe* I felt I had unhinged and deranged the novel from any inherited English context. Focussing on tiny details permitted long voyages both inside yet far beyond England and Europe, towards other life worlds. When I took to discussing the figure of Bloom in *Ulysses* I also lighted on tiny details and fragments, which again became the occasion for long voyages. Bloom was a character in a novel I was analysing. He also became a kind of doppelganger, my companion, my friend. Like Bloom I wanted to be all of Odysseus, Harun al-Rashid and Sindbad. Bloom's shouting out the name of Spinoza, a detail revealing whether or not Bloom was circumcised, a passage of Bloom's inner thought referring to the Biblical story of Exodus—these became the occasions for journeys into Spinoza as a Marrano and his heretical critiques of Judeo-Christianity, and into critiques of the Biblical stories as they related to Exodus and circumcision. I decided, nervously, the child of atheistical parents, that I had to read the Biblical stories for myself, and became fascinated by and drawn towards and into the language of the King James

Bible. Much of the book was written during this odd theological turn, an obsession which was perhaps thankfully supplanted towards the end by an interest in a new field, 'world history'.

In deranging texts from any usual textual treatment and context and field of intertextuality, I felt one has to take risks, one has to derange oneself, make sideways moves, go over the top and keep going, journey deep within oneself. One has to cultivate method as a kind of art of madness, even to the point of having a tattoo speak at the end of a chapter, provoking one, offering an alternative view. In dealing with 'world history'—with the many histories entwined in '1492', with critiques of Biblical stories like Exodus which can be recognised as foundational narratives in European and Western colonial societies,[13] with figures that might be considered exotic like the *conversos* and *Marranos* (*conversos* who were secret Jews) of sixteenth-century Portugal—my language had to mix parody and self-parody with something of the exaggeration, bombast and agonised violence of style that Benjamin says characterises the baroque theatre, literature and art of the seventeenth century. I have produced an example already, when I grandiloquently declared that Europe is an accursed continent. Benjamin says that the excess of baroque, appearing to be a caricature of classical tragedy, was conventionally considered for a long time, until modernism and especially early twentieth-century German Expressionism, to be offensive, even barbaric, to refined taste. Yes, I thought, pondering this, one sometimes has to be prepared to be barbaric, to feel that one does not have to be ruled by inherited modes, by a laconic Australian style or ideals of English understatement.

It was only in the long final year of revising, in the millennial liminality of 1999, that I worked out what the book was doing. I had constructed *1492* as an assemblage of journeys at once intellectual and fantastical: into literary and cultural history; into autobiography and family ancestry and stories; into the body and ethnic and cultural identity; into a methodology that seeks a kind of derangement; and into a rather bizarre theology. The various journeys themselves would have to be the interest of the book, not arriving at Ithaka, at anything resembling a secure identity or sense of belonging or certainty of argument or set of definite conclusions. I concluded that I should not have a conventional conclusion, but an anti-conclusion, various unrelated or clusters of loosely related reflections and observations and confessions of minor vagaries and fetishes—recalling my doppelganger Mr Bloom, though one could not hope to match Mr Bloom's range and accomplishment in this area. I called the anti-conclusion Concluding Mosaic.

ENDNOTES

1 G. Pandey, 'In Defense of the Fragment: Writing About Hindu-Muslim Riots in India Today', *Representations*, no. 37, 1992, p. 50.

2 See P. Hulme, 'Dire Straits: Ten Leagues Beyond', paper for conference on 'National Culture(s)', University of Casablanca, Ain Chok, November 1998.

3 E. Shohat, 'Staging the Quincentenary: The Middle East and the Americas', *Third Text*, 21, 1992–93, pp. 95–105. See also Y. Yovel, *The Marrano of Reason*, Princeton University Press, Princeton, 1989, pp. ix, 7, 15–17, 24–25, 54, 91, 189.

4 R. Fletcher, *Moorish Spain*, Phoenix, London, 1994, pp. 6–10, 172.

5 24 March 1994.

6 A. Alcalay, *After Jews and Arabs: Remaking Levantine Culture*, University of Minnesota Press, Minneapolis, 1993. See also S.D. Goitein, *Letters of Medieval Jewish Traders*, Princeton University Press, Princeton, 1974.

7 A. Ghosh, *In an Antique Land*, Granta/Penguin, London, 1994, pp. 19, 237. See also J. Clifford, *Routes: Travel and Translation in the Late Twentieth Century*, Harvard University Press, Cambridge, Mass., 1997, chapter 10, and E. Shohat, 'Taboo Memories and Diasporic Visions: Columbus, Palestine and Arab Jews', in M. Joseph and J. Fink (eds), *Performing Hybridity*, University of Minnesota Press, Minneapolis, 1999, pp. 131–56.

8 See also J. Docker, 'An Unbecoming Australian: Romancing a Lost Pre-1492 World', in R. Nile and M. Peterson (eds), *Becoming Australia: The Woodford Forum*, University of Queensland Press, St Lucia, 1998, pp. 136–48. Concerning food, cf. S.W. Mintz, *Tasting Food, Tasting Freedom: Excursions into Eating, Culture, and the Past*, Beacon Press, Boston, 1996, p. 68, on the importance in all known societies of 'ingestion as an arena for the classification and acting-out of moral principles' — or bizarre fantasies, he could have added.

9 J.S. Gerber, *The Jews of Spain: A History of the Sephardic Experience*, Free Press, New York, 1992.

10 W. Benjamin, *The Origin of German Tragic Drama*, trans. John Osborne, Verso, London, 1996, pp. 28, 32, 35, 44–47. Cf. A. Curthoys and J. Docker, 'Time, Eternity, Truth, and Death: History as Allegory', *Humanities Research*, no. 1, 1999, pp. 10–15.

11 See M. Rodinson, 'Recherches sur les documents arabes relatifs à la cuisine', *Revue des Etudes Islamiques*, 1949, pp. 95–165. See also B. Santich, *The Original Mediterranean Cuisine: Medieval Recipes for Today*, Wakefield Press, Adelaide, 1995, and R. Kabbani, 'Behind Him Lay the Great City of Cordoba', *Third Text*, vol. 6, no. 21, 1992, pp. 67–70.

12 E.W. Said, *The World, The Text, and the Critic*, Vintage, London, 1991, p. 253.

13 Cf. A. Curthoys, 'Expulsion, Exodus and Exile in White Australian Historical Mythology', *Journal of Australian Studies*, no. 61, 1999, issue on Imaginary Homelands, edited by R. Nile and M. Williams, pp. 1–18.

CHAPTER 5

○ FANTASY UPON ONE NOTE

Peter Read

In July 1997 as part of a project comparing the destroyed places of several overseas areas with those of Australia, I visited Croatia with a friend who had been born near the town of Split on the Adriatic coast. I was overwhelmed by its history: the Croatians' precise and bitter memories of the Second World War, the scores of historic monuments defaced or destroyed by succeeding generations of invaders, the former use of public signage to reinforce political ideology, the abrupt proximity of so many invasions and wars, the savagery of recent fighting, the intense passions about the communist past, the ancient rituals and cycles of peasant life in the little village of Cevoglave which seemed to have been let slip only yesterday. The emotional keystone of the trip was a day-long journey, escorted and guided by people from the Croatian Ministry of Culture through some of the regions of the recently pacified and physically devastated war zones.[1]

In the course of a career in indigenous history of many thousands of conversations and hundreds of visits, I have stood before more than one massacre site and absorbed countless horror stories from victims of the stolen generations. When the trip was over my friend, the Australian Research Council Small Grants Committee and the Croatian Ministry of Culture all expected something from me. After some deliberation I decided to write about my tour of the war zone. But how? My heart beat faster every time I thought about it. I began to realise that I was still deeply traumatised by the status merely of bystander. The enduring destructive physicality of the Croatian war—my experience of mile after mile of destroyed countryside, murdered people and ruined towns—affected me in ways that I did not expect and even now cannot easily express. My memories of that midsummer day of 1997 seemed almost too overwhelming to put into prose. Into what parameters would I sort my emotions as I stood in the ruined museum of the Jacenovac World War II concentration camp: the door shot in, the flagpole smashed, the garden trampled, machine gun bullets across the ceiling, huge black and white photographs of murdered men and women hanging ripped in half from the walls. How could I mentally accommodate the excavations carried out in the stinking local rubbish tip to find and identify the human bones thrown in along with those of pig and sheep to hide the whereabouts of killed civilians; the woman who discovered her missing husband in the well when she caught the smell of his decaying corpse; the black and stinking penises of dead soldiers sent back to the enemy in cardboard boxes. How can we historians encompass such deeds, sinister and savage, heinous and unspeakable, and, most of all, deeds incomprehensible? What words can apprehend the inexplicable? Can the very act of writing shape the emotional response? Such is the ancient *cri de coeur* expressed by Rilke and later by Drusilla Modjeska: 'Help me, in saying it, to understand it.'[2]

Some days or weeks after 31 August 1680 Henry Purcell wrote a fantasy for five viols, 'Upon One Note'.[3] A fantasy was the English version of free but brief improvisation, a form much in vogue among Elizabethan composers but becoming old-fashioned by the Restoration. Also almost obsolete were the intimate performances of a chest of viols, the rather twangling family of stringed instruments, former competitors to the violin family but more limited in dynamics and range, which were becoming superseded by this time.[4] Purcell himself did not particularly like them, evidently thinking them rather nasal and harsh. Yet in 1680, at the age of 22, he wrote a miraculous set of fantasias for viols. As was still the English custom, he scored them for three, four or five equal parts. Though relatively unknown except among chamber musicians, I've always admired them for their conciseness, their harmonic daring, their measured melancholy, most of all for their exquisite sense of structure and form.

I came across Purcell's fantasies in the early 1970s when I was learning to play the bass viol, under the tuition of Francis and June Baines, in early music classes held in Chiswick, London. Francis led the Jaye Consort of Viols, then a well known English ensemble. Sooner or later beginners like me were introduced to a particular fantasy from the set entitled 'Upon One Note', because the middle player of the five parts plays nothing but the note F throughout the entire piece. At bar 25 the one-noter even plays an eerie solo, just for a quaver; at bar 27 the player has a whole minim while the other players are silent! The four other parts are usually played by two treble viols, a tenor and a bass.[5] In performance, the Jaye consort used to play the bottom line on a wonderfully reverberating seven-string bass made in 1606 by the famous Renaissance instrument maker, Henry Jaye, himself.

In my imagined perfect performance, Purcell's fantasy Upon One Note emerges out of several seconds of total silence. In the first bar, the keynote F already assumed by the middle part, the bass rises meditatively up the F major scale. It's joined by the second tenor an octave above. In the second bar the first of the treble viols begins a descending identical scale. In the third bar the second treble and the first of the tenors diverge equally, again from F. The bass begins the pattern again and brings the introduction to a sonorous close at the beginning of the seventh bar. Now emerges a seven-bar development, still slow, built on a dotted rhythm. In the third section—we are less than a minute into the piece—the emotional tension warms from meditative to thoughtful. Half a minute later, now in the fourth, Purcell doubles the time in a brief phrase for all the instruments (except the one-noter), the parts tripping, skipping, interrupting, tossing higher and higher. Just four bars later comes the fifth, a longer phrase embraced by all the parts, three times the tempo of the introduction. We are more than half-way through the piece. At this point, marked 'Slow', Purcell pulls us to reflection in grinding chromatic runs which must have sounded strange indeed to the court of Queen Mary. Abruptly in the sixth section, we are thrown into semi-quavers, four times the original tempo, another tiny phrase, tumbling, grasping, searching, thrusting higher and higher until at bar 40 the first treble shouts a dotted rhythm against the other equal parts, the snatched soaring climax of a high C. At once the pace slows. Down a long descending run, in the exact same seven-bar sequence with which the fantasy began, we glide from semi-quavers to quavers to crochets to minims: E flat, D, C, B natural, B flat, A natural, A flat, G and at last the welcoming, resolving F held by all the instruments, not even a full F major chord, for all but one of the instruments are holding the tonic.

That last chord lingers for two meditative bars. The slowing, diminishing but purposeful descent into the nothingness out of which the piece emerged ends the tiny apocalypse. The seven sections of this minor miracle of English music would make an apt funeral elegy for those who believe that life emerges out of silence, builds on its own past, allows and demands time for meditation, holds its own seasons and cross rhythms, carries lesser climaxes within its crescendos, and concedes that there may be time only for a brief but elegant farewell.

Much learned discussion has compared the structures and techniques of musical composition to those of writing, but the attempted close analogies between prose and counterpoint, tonality, ground bass, dissonance, suspension, variation and cross-rhythm I find more interesting than convincing. Yet this fantasy has never ceased to touch me both as a music lover and as a writer. I embrace its balanced form, its planned ascending emotional peaks, its solemn exuberance, its brevity, its dynamic tension, its controlled cyclic acceptance, its elegance.

Help me, in saying it, to understand it. The fantasy Upon One Note helped me to formulate those unquiet, unshaped experiences of the Croatian war. The article I would write would be the journey itself, the narrative structure, the events of that single day, a piece unrolling as the experiences themselves unrolled from dawn to dusk. It would be called 'A Day in the Country with Dr Death', for I had seen this name of a heavy metal band inscribed, I think disingenuously, in white paint on the useless electronic scoreboard of the destroyed bowling alley in the blown-up health resort of the Liptik Compleks. The emotional control of the fantasy could discipline my experiences as a series of rising emotional climaxes. Each site confronted would be more appalling than the previous: the dawn dim and cool, then warmer, hot, hotter, blazing hot, cooling, at last to a descent into the plain in the cool dusk of evening. The fantasy could show me how to shape, direct and order the experiences as a first stage of bringing myself to the point where I *could* write about them. Purcell would enable me to be my own therapist, not simply by copying his own musical plan (an exercise not only pointless but inimical to artistic intuition); no, an artistic structure—in this case, musical—could frame my powerful, undigested emotions into a kind of comprehension. I could not come to terms with what I had confronted until, as it were, I could format them.

Mindful of the power of Purcell's strong sectionalised concision, I arranged my response—then the article—into cumulative, short, terse paragraphs:

> We begin our day in the country with Dr Death at Korita. Korita used to be a village of a hundred people, some 150 kms east of Zagreb. Now it is a collection of ruined houses. At the time of our visit, the gardens are quite wild in the hot mid morning of high summer. Fences are overthrown, the gardens are empty. Graves have vanished in the undergrowth.

In the second section I worked out my sense of violent irony:

> At the foot of the range lies the town of Pakrac … [where] one memorial to the suffering may remain unnoticed and unrepaired. In the town square is a bronze monument of the Second World War. It is a sculpture of a man *in extremis*, a dying Yugoslav soldier. His battle jacket is torn off and half gone. His head is thrown backwards, his ribs protrude horribly, his body arches to breaking point. But he and the plinth on which he lies dying are now pocked and holed by shrapnel.

The third section occurred at the peak of the fiery day:

> The temperature has risen to 95 degrees as we drive to Jasenovac. It is the site of the infamous concentration camp where at least 60 000 Serbs perished at the hands of the Croatian Ustashe during the Second World War.

The fourth echoed the sense of a cumulating and barely comprehensible violence:

> Worse follows ... The fifty six people [of the village of Hvratska Kostjanjica] who answered the summons to an evening meeting were so little prepared for what was to come that they came with handbags or umbrellas ... The fifty six were loaded onto trucks, taken to a green rolling meadow only two kilometres from the town and shot with machine guns. How familiar this lovely site must have been to the villagers, how often they must have visited. And how small a hole it needs to hold fifty-six bodies.

Purcell inserted his reflective passage—perhaps he saw it as a keystone—in the middle of his fantasy. My more personal reflection on the Yugoslavian tragedy seemed to fall naturally at the end. We ascended a high hill on a obscure and shell-holed road to a group of four or five houses, all destroyed:

> I clamber through a ground level window of a three storey house. Broken concrete, smashed tile; stair without railing, pot plant without water, garden without nurture, window without glass, verandah without chairs, walls without pictures, door frames without door, playroom without toys, kitchen without warmth, table without conversation, bedroom without love.

And now to apply the brake to bring myself a slower, more gentle but purposeful closure:

> beyond the ash trees and down the hill, the full sun of the Croatian summer is gold in the dying light. Chimneys and factories, chequerboard farms, darker forests, fading red roofs, fading white walls, fading streets, fading communities, dead towns. Night closed over what will not be apprehended even in broad daylight: mourning, grief, trauma, desolation, absence. Tragedy for everyone touched by this savage war, the unrequited passions which swim and hover in the cooling evening air.

I don't think anyone much liked the piece, though I still can't read it without emotion. The Ministry of Culture was lukewarm, I suppose because they thought it rather unpolitical. I had trouble placing it in one or two overseas newspapers and in the end was content with *Arena*.[6] That no one else seemed particularly moved by my essay doesn't worry me very much. Purcell enabled me to give my thoughts a structure, and I know now that I was writing out my trauma as a kind of therapy. Purcell gave me a frame to do it. Art structured emotion, then emotion structured art.

ENDNOTES

1   I suspect that my companion had billed me to the Croatian authorities as more of a political writer than I am or want to be.

2   Quoted by D. Modjeska as an epigraph of *Stravinsky's Lunch*, Picador, Sydney, 1999.

3   In the collection are thirteen fantasies, and two In Nomines. The first twelve are dated, the last as 31 August 1680. The fantasy 'Upon One Note' is the only one undated.

4   The best known of the viol family is that for which Marin Marais wrote many works, the viola da gamba ('knee viol'), which is played like a cello, but supported not by a spike on the floor, but on the calves. Historically viols were constructed in many sizes, but all, except the largest basses, were supported on the lap or the calves.

5   Composers of chamber music often did not specify which member of the viol family was to play which part; it is today not unusual for different instruments, such as viols and recorders, to take different parts to form a broken consort.

6   P. Read, 'A Day in the Country With Dr Death', *Arena Magazine*, no. 33, 1998, pp. 6–8.

CHAPTER 6

○ WRITING: PRAXIS AND PERFORMANCE

Greg Dening

'Non-fiction' is a word that bugs me. I don't write 'non' anything. And I don't like the company I am forced to keep on the 'non-fiction' shelves in the bookstores, or on the best-sellers lists (in my dreams!)—cookbooks, personality disorders, do-it-yourselves, ghost-written autobiographies of sporting stars.

Maybe I don't have a word to replace 'non-fiction'. These days I tend to describe myself as a writer of true stories. I'd settle for having my books on a shelf called 'Creative Writing', though. I should, of course, buy my own bookstore and label my shelves for myself. Virtual Reality and Reality? Fantasy and Fiction? No, for this exercise, I'll settle for Creative Writing. Let's talk about writing our true stories with creative imagination.

Imagination scares many scholars. They equate it with fantasy. But imagination is not really fantasy. Imagination is catching a glimpse of the end of the trail before we make the first step. Imagination is finding a word that someone else will hear, a metaphor that someone else will see. Imagination is seeing what's absent, hearing the silence as well as the noise. Imagination is taking the cliché out of what has been said over and over again. Imagination is taking the purpose of the rules that confine us and running with it. Imagination is working the fictions in our non-fiction the better to do what we want to do with our writing.

One of the things that I want to do with my writing is to change the world in some way—little ways, politically, culturally, socially, intellectually. I can't change the past. I can't give life to the dead. I can't give justice to the victims. But I can change the world with my true stories. Well, I can try!

I'm a story-teller. I can't force people to read my stories. I have to persuade them first to open my book, then to read the first sentence, and the next. No one is paid to read my stories. Ah, now, there's a point. For most of us beginning a writing career by 'doing' history, by 'doing' a PhD, our readers—our examiners, our supervisors—are paid to read what we write. For the most part, these paid readers don't have to be persuaded that what we write is important or worth reading. For most of them, their reading is determined by their own expertise and their relationship to us.

Real writing is different. No one is paid to read it. Let's talk about creative imagination and real writing. Let's make a resolution not to 'do' a thesis, but to write a book. This won't be a book that will certainly be published. Not many of us have that assurance. Let's write a book in the sense that our readers will be more than three in number, and won't be as expert as we are in our topic. Let's decide that we are writers, story-tellers, not 'doers' of theses.

Many of us will feel uncomfortable with that decision. Many will think that there is a contradiction between creative imagination and 'doing' a thesis. That is, 'doing' a thesis has many explicit rules that have to be obeyed and many more implicit rules that we disobey only at great risk. Many will feel that the time to be creative is after the thesis has been done.

It would be irresponsible for me to ride roughshod over such concerns. So let me make some serious statements.

1. You have the freedom to let your creativity work so long as you explicitly and consciously display why you are extending the rules or apparently breaking them. You have freedom so long as you display the advantages and disadvantages of doing something different. The rules are your protection. Part of your examination is knowing how and when the rules are applicable. Your freedom is dependent on your being your own examiner and showing that you do or don't do things with purpose, and not out of ignorance.

2. The greatest freedom that you have is in the creative structure with which you present the whole of your book. There is no need to follow slavishly such customs as an Introduction, six Chapters and a Conclusion, so long as you fulfil all the functions that such customs are meant to perform. The more you signpost the whole with its internal continuities, its parts, its clusters of significant chapters, its different voices, its different functions, the better.

3. Whatever way you conceive of your readers as more than examiners, you will have much to learn from novelists, playwrights, film-makers, poets, about writing directly, experientially and reflectively.

4. You won't have creative freedom unless you have an effective note-taking system that leaves you in control of the vast amount of data you will have accumulated. Experience tells me that you will require two note-taking systems. One will let you retrieve the discursive elements of what you read—its structure of presentation, its relationships to other texts, its bibliographic detail, your reactions to what you read. The other will allow you to re-shape these discursive notes into their significance for you. For a major project I would normally have a pile of discursive notes half a metre high and more. At frequent intervals as I stock that pile, I reconstruct it into notes that tell me the significance of

every note that I have taken. I return to the whole pile more than once. I don't begrudge the three or four weeks it takes to re-structure it all together. I work better with A4 pages than with small cards. Each page has a category or subject title and I pull out from all over my discursive notes the information relevant to that title, being very careful to have a secure and accurate referencing system. I aim to have the whole pile of discursive notes in my head in a memorable way.

5. Enjoy the freedom of writing titles and sub-titles for your work and all its parts. Avoid 'what' and topic titles—'Settlement at Botany Bay', 'Causes of Pacific Exploration'. Write dynamic titles that really indicate what it is that you are trying to say or want the reader to understand. Try the present participle, '-ing' words. 'Settling Botany Bay', 'The Greed and Glory of Going Further'.

6. Nothing is written until it is read. Get a reader. Don't get possessive of what you have written. If your reader doesn't understand what you have written or takes it in the wrong way, it's you who have to change, not them.

*   *   *

Writing fills the hours of my days and the years of my life. It is a privileged time for me. I am more writer than professor, I would say, except that being a professor, professing who I am and how I want to change the world, is, in my mind, being a writer. But these days I am just as likely to be asked to read what I have written as much as lecture. I enjoy reading aloud and in public what I have written. In any case, I read aloud what I have written to myself, and encourage every young writer to do the same. I discover the awkwardnesses of my expression in reading aloud. I catch the rhythm of my style, or the lack of it. I periodise what I have written with silences the better for hearing them. I develop theatre in the abrupt phrases and epigrammatic signing-offs.

Reading aloud, even privately, is something of an indulgence, I know. And it is not the way that most people will read my writing. But you have to be an honest reader to be a writer, I like to say. You have to know your own modes of reading, when you skim, how you skim. I know for myself that my eye very likely will skim to the bottom of an indented, single spaced, smaller font quotation. As a writer, I avoid indented paragraphs like the plague. I either make the quotation in full with the same style as all the other paragraphs, or I break it up and incorporate its images and phrases into my own narrative.

Honesty tells me that I rarely read a book in one sitting. Even when I am lucky it can take three weeks. As a reader, remembering what I've read and keeping the continuities going is a problem. As a writer, I need tricks to keep the reader's attention. I know that in a large manuscript I don't easily remember what I have written. It takes a reader to see immediately some phrase that I have repeated. Broken reading of large manuscripts means that the reader needs memory stations. I find that encapsulating my narrative in a metaphor that surfaces at crucial points acts as memory stations for the reader, takes them back to what they have read.

Honesty tells me that the white spaces on a page affect my responses to what I read. The aesthetics of my page is part of my writing, the length of a line, the size of a paragraph. Honesty tells me that mostly my eyes are well ahead of my mind in reading, or that I read not one word at a time but in gulps of sentences and paragraphs and even of pages. Honesty tells me that I rarely read every sentence in a book. Honesty tells me that I will reduce the tens of thousands of words in a book to twenty or thirty or a hundred to say what it means. As a writer, my strategy is to control those few words.

Honesty tells me that I find most captions to illustrations a bore. I want my visual imaging to work with my text. I want my images to be another sort of narrative. So I wrap them around with discursive texts. I'm sceptical about the effectiveness of boxed images with bare captions. So I try to make image essays. Really I would like to forego the concept of 'illustration' altogether. I want my images to be another sort of text.

These days I'm shaping a book that I'm calling *Beach Crossings*. I can't read it aloud for you. Maybe you can read it aloud for yourself. It is an unusual invitation, I know. But I am talking Praxis and Performance. The days are gone, I think, when writers can hide behind their nervousness at public performance. Words aren't just things on paper, or in the mind. We are writers in all parts of our bodies. In any case, 'just do it'. I dare you to read me aloud.

BEACH CROSSINGS: A READING WITH TWO VOICES (YOURS AND MINE)

'This is not a book', Paul Gauguin protests in the first sentence of *Avant et Après*. In the last months of his life, he had turned to words rather than paint. But he struggles with words, doesn't want to be judged by them. 'This is not a book', he repeats mantra-like at each moment he expects his reader to be exacerbated by his discontinuities, whenever he presents himself brazenly as he is, without persuasion, without style, without art. Not a book, 'scattered notes, unconnected, like dreams, like life, made of bits and pieces'.

But the bits and pieces of his life as he sees it now at the end of it are framed by the *Before and After* of his beach crossings on the margins of the civilised world.

Gauguin is writing this 'naked, fearless, shameless' self-portrait in the top floor of his *Maison du Plaisir*, his 'House of Orgasm'. His 'House of Orgasm' is an island on an island. Cyclone and flood have divided it off from the little village of Atuona on Hiva Oa in the Marquesas. It is January 1903. Gauguin had used this top-storey room as his studio for eighteen months. It is cluttered and disordered, a lumber room of special woods, a museum of finished and unfinished carvings and sculptures. There is a harmonium in the centre, an easel by the open window at the northern end. Padlocked chests and sets of drawers filled with prints and drawings. The walls are hung with eclectic reproductions of art—Hans Holbein, Albrecht Dürer, Pierre Puvis de Chavannes, Edgar Degas. Photographs of Parthenon friezes and Asian temples are hung there too. Gauguin always believed that the history of art and of cultures flowed through his fingers to his canvasses.

His bedroom, accessed by a ladder he can now barely climb, was the threshold to his studio. There the walls were hung with photographs of his family, and a collection of lewd photographs he had purchased in Port Said. Gauguin would fondle and caress the women of the island as they ogled and laughed at the postures and contortions. It was a House of Orgasm after all.

In these last days he set his painting of a Breton snow scene on an easel at the foot of his bed. It would have been the last thing he saw before he died. The snow scene was an icon of his Before, a reminder of how twenty years before he had challenged the virtuosity of Monet and Courbet with his colours. He loved the edgelessness that colour gave to lines. Colour gave a dreamlike quality to shapes. When colours merged, sharpness had no space of its own. Defining lines were a trick of the eye. The trickster in the painter made it so. That is what Gauguin knew in the Before of his career. In the After of his beach, Gauguin now knew that edgelessness was not just a trick of the eye. On his beach, Gauguin had experienced a different order of things. The defining lines of the Before of his civilised world were gone in the wildness of his savage After. His older divisions between human and divine, living and dead, male and female, child and adult, landscape and person were blurred now. There was a clutter of paintings in his studio, and packages of them in transport at sea to show it.

Gauguin cannot stand at his easel any more. The pain in his ulcerated legs is too great even with the morphine. He is breathless with angina. His syphilis is taking away his eyesight. His eyes look piggy behind the steel rimmed circles of his spectacles. He knows he will not paint for much longer. He knows he is dying. His last painting has a realism his others don't possess. He paints himself as dead man looking. He throws away all the disguises of his other self-portraits and sets himself drawn with pain, dried-up with discontents. 'Koke', 'Wattle-Daub', the islanders called him. Koke was his *patiki*, the shit name of a first tattoo. Gauguin's suppurating skin peeled away like grey rendering on a wall. The sight and smell of it had driven the sex out of his life, had driven everyone away, everyone save one who was bound to him in a special way on his beach.

That one was Tioka, 'Scooped-Out'. 'Wattle-Daub' and 'Scooped-Out' had a special relationship. They had exchanged names. Exchanging names like Wattle-Daub and Scooped-Out might not seem to have much aesthetic appeal. The exchange was a social grace nonetheless. The mutual gift of names embraced the whole person, all the person's rights and obligations, the property. It was never given lightly. It was given between equals but not necessarily between identicals. There was barter in it. Different advantages were exchanged. It was empowering, though. It was political, an alliance in the grassroots of life. It was an alliance steeped as well in all the cultural memories of how things used to be. Exchanging names was a very proper sacrament of beach crossings.

Tioka it was who found Koke dead in his bed, the body still warm, an empty morphine syringe beside it. It was 11.00 am, 8 May 1903. The Church with graceless haste performed all the proprieties for Koke's launch into eternity. There would have been no great confidence that holy water, oil and prayer would do their work. Koke would have been happier with Tioka's last rite. It had a savage, even cannibal, feel. Tioka bit Koke's skull in hope of some resurrection, in release of a troubled and troubling spirit.

✻ ✻ ✻

It is not for me to say what you see and feel in what I write. Let me give some advice on writing and you can see for yourself whether I take my own advice.

Be Mysterious. 'Mystery', 'mysterious', are words layered with thousands of years of meaning. At the heart of these meanings is an understanding that a mystery is the most complicated truth clothed in story or play or sacramental sign. Being mysterious means that there is work to be done—not just by the story-teller, not just by the author, not just by the priest, but by the audience, the reader, the believer as well. There is no closure to mysteries, only another story, another translation. I think that a writer should liberate the readers to go where they want. It is their conversation that we are joining. There is a certain abruptness or directness in being mysterious. We have to have the confidence that readers have instantaneous skills in being where we take them.

Be Experiential. We write with authority when we write as observers. Not as spectators, but as observers. Our own honesty is at stake as observers. As observers our cultural antennae are at their peak. Every trivial detail is larger than itself in an observation. We see the interconnectedness of things. We read the gestures with the same astuteness that we need to have to survive culturally in everyday life. We are seeing the multiple meanings in every word. We are catching meaning in the context of the occasion. Above all, as observers we are reflective. We see ourselves mirrored in our own observations. We know our honesty. We know our uncertainties. We know our tricks. Be experiential in your writing and the reader will come with you.

Be Compassionate. It is awfully easy for an historian not to be compassionate. I sometimes think that this is because we write in the past tense and with hindsight. Try writing what you have written in the past tense in the present tense and you will see what I mean. Suddenly you have to know so much more. Suddenly the perspective is forward and not backward. We don't have to write in the present tense though to be compassionate. What we have to do is to give its own present tense back to the past we are writing about. We give back to the past its own possibilities, its own ambiguities, its own incapacity to see the consequences of its action. It is only then that we represent what actually happened.

Be Entertaining. I am using the word 'entertaining' in its etymological sense of 'holding between', *enter tenere* in the Latin. Think of all the tricks we use in the theatre to hold the gaze and attention of an audience—darkened theatre, stage curtains, the triangular perspective of the stage. We have to find ways to entertain our readers in the same way. I suspect that if we watch novelists, playwrights and film directors entertaining their audiences we will find that they have more courage to be direct than we usually do. We take a hundred steps back to make one jump and keep shouting 'I'm coming! I'm coming!' Readers can cope with a lot more directness and silence.

Be Performative. There is no such thing as a perfect performance. A performance is always limited in some way—by a stage-call, by a deadline, by a word limit. Performance is always heralded by a risk-taking. That is why it is different from practice. A performance is before somebody. We always know in a performance how we have gone. The whole family out there might say we were wonderful, but in performance we are our own critics. In performance, the risk-taking is often breaking through the formalism that limits us. In performance we can't live by the formalities of the rules, we have to live by the meaning of the rules. We have to take the rules further to make them work. I'm thinking of referencing, footnoting and all the paraphernalia that surrounds academic writing. It is the function and purpose of the rule that needs to be obeyed, not their literal interpretation.

✻   ✻   ✻

Most of us will become a world expert on our topic of research within three or four months of beginning it. After three or four months we will have more about our topic in our head than anyone else in the world. The only trouble is that no one else wants all that knowledge in their head too. What they want is for us to join a conversation that they are already having. We need to know where the conversations around us have been coming from. We need to have the desire to take them further.

An important part of writing is re-writing. The computer is a wonderful tool for a writer, but it doesn't help re-writing. We sometimes can't bear to cut a paragraph that we've put so much time in sculpting and typing. We try to find a place for it somewhere else. Believe me, you can see a replaced paragraph. Don Watson, Paul Keating's speech-writer and a script-writer himself, says that the key to re-writing is reduction. What you put in ten lines, reduce to five; five to two. I do most of my re-writing as I write. I am always turning to the beginning of a sentence and asking myself, does it intrigue a reader to read on. On the larger scale, I doubt if I have ever finished a book in less than seven or eight major drafts.

I tell my students that when they have finished a draft that they are reasonably happy with they should make an index. Just a name and place index itself will be helpful. They will find how inconsistent they have been in spelling and referencing. They will find important additions that they must make—in initials or first names before surnames, for example. More importantly they should make a subject index, a detailed analytic map of their thinking. An index of their thinking will give them confidence, because they will see how they embroider their concepts. They will make important discoveries about themselves and how they can re-adjust what they have written for more clarity or more persuasiveness.

The computer, as I have said, has given us an aesthetic for our writing. These days I do not give a manuscript to the publisher until I have made a mock-up of the book I want to see. I use some desktop publication software. *Pagemaker* has always suited me. I wouldn't hand a thesis in these days without having done something similar.

I don't like the word 'theory' when it is associated with the history we are writing. Too often 'theory' is seen as a sort of template to superimpose on historical events and circumstances. The irrelevance of 'theory' is seen most often in an introductory 'theory' chapter. Very often this is the last time enlarging concepts, contextualising perceptions and cross-disciplinary insights are displayed in an extended piece of writing. The 'theory' chapter may as well have not been written.

I'm more comfortable with the word 'reflection'. Narrative and reflection are, for me, two sides of the same coin of historical writing. Reflection is a self-consciousness about what one is doing as a writer and observer. Reflection is joining the sentences of what I am saying to the conversation someone else is having. Reflection is, as I have written before, plumbing the depths of our own plagiarism.

Reflection is most effective when it is woven into the narrative, but we can pull it out of the narrative in all sorts of ways so long as its attachment to our narrative is clear, and readers don't feel that they are being dragged off on some paper chase.

Sometimes the relation between narrative and reflection is an awkward one. We intrude on our narrative and say what our story means. This can be counter-productive. Our story-telling should be so skilful that we don't have to say what it means.

I call this the theatre of our history-writing. If we go to the theatre, we don't expect the playwright to appear on the stage and tell us what the play means. In a play, we hear the most trivial remarks about totally particularised things. We, the audience, have no difficulty in going out into the foyer and telling one another what the play meant. If we write well, the meaning that readers see in our writing will also be ours, signposted in all sorts of ways.

*   *   *

I want to change the world with my writing, I say. Well, maybe just to get the world to laugh or cry or be serious for a moment. A few years ago, as the HIV epidemic took hold, the Commonwealth government had an advertising campaign. Death, as Father Time, played ten-pin bowling with human lives. We saw men, women and children scattered randomly with his bowls. There was a great deal of critical comment at what was seen as scare-mongering propaganda. Surveys were taken as to its effectiveness. The only concrete effect that could be noted, however, was that membership of ten-pin bowling clubs dropped!

That is a depressing story for anyone wanting to change the world with their writing. I have to warn you that the pleasure of writing is more in the doing of it than in any grandiose sense of power. The pleasure of writing, for me, has always been the discovery of what is in my mind. I don't like to talk about what I am writing at any particular time. Talking about it lessens the sense of surprise I like to have at any thought or phrase that is in my head. There are a few days after I have finished a piece of writing, when my mind is still racing, when I like to savour what I have written by reading it over again. But, I used to say to my students, that waiting for the effects of what one has written is like dropping a stone into a deep well and waiting for the splash. No, it's not, said a friend. It is like dropping a rose petal into the Grand Canyon and expecting a bang!

The greatest pleasure that we have as writers is to hear from someone who has read us. That's my splash, at least. Knowing that, and knowing how short life is, I like to tell other writers of the splashes that they have made in my mind. That is the final praxis I would recommend to any young writer. Express your admiration for what others have done. That in itself is a performance.

CHAPTER 7

○ REFLEXIVITY AND THE SELF-LINE

Ann McGrath

BEGINNINGS

A few years ago, I wrote a letter to Greg Dening. I was staying at my childhood home in Brisbane, where my parents still live. It was the school vacation, and my daughters were being minded upstairs by their grandparents. I sat in the office under the house, a 1950s-style elevated Queensland house, not the romantic now sought-after variety with deep wooden verandahs, but one with a concrete patio and swirly wrought iron railing up a tiled staircase. Under the house was not a place for us children, at least on weekdays. This was the office and base of the family plumbing business—one side housed a row of plumbing vans which seeped black liquid onto the concrete ground, while above hung the ingeniously arranged, ever changing complex of copper and plastic pipes. Like branches of a familiar canopy, these softly gleaming creatures went unnoticed by me, though it was hard to ignore the racket of their clanging early-morning departures from beneath my bedroom floorboards. Under the house, the brick wall on the far side was lined with cardboard box after box of plumbing taps, washers, sockets, tools, hot-water systems, drain-digging devices, and the 'Insinkerator' cutting tool Dad had invented himself: anonymous brown boxes, except for the scrawled, indecipherable abbreviations and bad spelling. The place I wrote that letter was in the office, with its sour, peppery smells of metals, burning solder, grease, raw bricks and mortar, and its distracting poster of 'unionist' monkeys dressed as plumbers. This narrow, cave-like room was now devoted to charity work, especially speeches for the Lions Club.

Enjoying the powerful sense of reunion with my past self which I experience every time my eyes and being connect with Brisbane and the continuity of the family home, I had been working on a paper for a History conference which recalled my first experience of giving birth. The story of the birth of my eldest daughter, Venetia, eight years before, had taken a long time before groping its way towards a written version. As part of my historical practice, I now wanted to explore the personal, partly to show how historians prohibit entry to their own personal experiences in their work, and partly to make my point about childbirth being an important experience for many woman, yet still omitted from history-writing.[1]

Rather than theorising about the 'why' of introducing the reflexive narrative at a historians' conference, I felt the message might be best *demonstrated* rather than argued, *performed* rather than theoretically examined. After an earlier foray into the reflexive, where I'd briefly explored aspects of growing up white and the ways my generation learnt about primitivity and Aborigines, one close colleague remarked the paper was very 'cultural studies-ish'—that is, not history. Another accused me of self-indulgence, selfishness, and other deadly sins of the self. Eventually I bounced back to figure I could be onto something; if what I was doing was so threatening, it must be worth doing more of. Perhaps it could even be leading towards the innovative.

It so happened I'd brought Greg Dening's *Performances* with me to Brisbane, and my children were having far too much fun to interrupt my absorption.[2] I recognised Dening's discussions of those most antagonistic to reflexivity and their need to clothe themselves in the theatre of earnest, stodgy prose. He grappled towards the reflexive voice: 'We have lost history when … authors cannot recognise or refuse to display their own presence' and '[A]uthorial presence is a political right in a postmodern world'.[3] I was thrilled by Dening's self-exploratory lyricism, the insights he shared with his luscious words. So, in between writing my emotional and female-centred journey, I wrote to Dening. I wanted to tell him of my joy, excitement and the way he'd inspired me with a new sense of creativity and the confidence to float around in it.

I did not send the letter. It was not quite complete. The prose seemed too humble, the tone too bereft of poetry. My letter must be worthy of its inspiration, its excitement, and it wasn't. I look at the letter again, examine it. Its ending about my imminent trip to the United States irritates me. It has no proper date. It was to be found only on an old desktop computer, which, having caught the millennium bug long ago, records the entire 1990s as '1904'. But I know the letter would have been written in 1996, probably August.

THE LETTER

Dear Professor Dening,

I thoroughly enjoyed your piece in *Australian Book Review* and also *Performances*, from which I've consumed numerous delectable meals, but which I'm trying desperately to shove aside in order to finish my [Australian Historical Association] paper. So much of what you say resonates very loudly with me. I love it and have been flying with it, and am wondering where to land.

In the past weeks I have been stumbling along wanting to say some of these things, some similar things, in my AHA paper; at this moment I feel inclined to give a whole paper just quoting you, geneflecting (spelling?) towards the lovely words and then preaching about how others should read them. One of the real delights in your book is to escape a certain sort of 'politics' and to enjoy the possibilities of wisdom through reflection and knowledge. You leave an expansive open-endedness about which direction to take this in.

The other thing which I'd like to talk to you about is the question of 'I' in the narrative. Yes, we have to be there to be postmodern, to live in our time, or we'll stay fundamentalists; that's why I liked the writing of Americans Patsy Nelson Limerick and Richard White[4] in their self-conscious revelations about their engagement in writing and research. But we can go further than that.

What struck me as unresolved or perhaps out of character in your writings, was your discomfort at accusations of 'self-indulgence' or 'arrogance' in the case of using yourself/oneself as a starting point—you went along with Wordsworth here.[5] It is as though you can debunk lots of other traditions but you are not sure in your own being that it is not true, that self-reflection is vanity. (Excuse unrefined prose, but there's the AHA paper!) This seems to hit on some big ethnographic questions; is this a Jesuit influence, an Australian thing, or more a history-discipline thing? While reading into counter-anthropology I thought the term 'navel-gazing' was a good put-down when I got fed up with where it was going, so I've been guilty of the sin of intolerance myself.[6] But a lot of people love reading about other people's thoughts and lives and how they got to be where they are. I'm one of them. Introductions and prologues can be more meaningful than the rest and we shouldn't maroon them on distant atolls. I'm not retired yet and therefore not in the acceptable autobiographical mode of this space, but the time has already come to contextualise my own experience as part of the reflection of the cultural history I write. For some years I've been looking for the affirmation around me to do this, and I feel I found it in your work. I was scared of being called self-indulgent. Exactly. Now I've already been called it [,] nastily [been] hurt by it, cried, then later realised it was the threatening nature of some of my prose to a 'dull and boring' gatekeeper of stodgy masculine 'scholarship' and [,] in the extremity of his reaction, better realised my purpose and if I again get called it I can now think of why before getting buffeted into desolation. There's a great courage needed in self-revelation and whilst I have some of this, I have a dreadful thin skin which defies change. And perhaps it's the ability to feel things which brings glimpses of quality to my writing.

So the reason I wrote this letter is that I wanted to thank you for the lovely experience of reading your words. I also wondered whether you might read some of mine (when ready) and offer advice. The book I'm working on is along the lines of Gendered Frontiers: Intercultural encounters in time. And finally, I'm off on a study leave trip to the US where I was planning to spend time at Yale and Johns Hopkins and wondered whether you'd recommend some people I should meet or places I should go. Several big 'asks' to end a letter originally intended to pay homage, but of course you can say no.

Yours sincerely

Ann McGrath

Why don't we include letters in our historical prose?
Diary entries?
Our own letters?
It took a while for the moment to come; now it's here[7]

THE CONFERENCE PAPER

Curiously, the letter mentions nothing at all about my current explorations into childbirth. In holding onto a kind of privacy, a refusal to 'come out', I didn't even name the subject of my paper. Was it too intimate for someone I didn't know, too female? Or was it not yet ready for the light? I harboured the hope that Greg might be there in Melbourne when I presented my paper.

Nervous to face the moment, the packed room was quiet, I ran over time. I ended with an exhortation about writing the births of a nation for federation, of exploring the spaces between metaphor and lived experience. I said historians like Simon Schama, Greg Dening, Gail Reekie and Ann Curthoys have called upon us to reflect more carefully upon the ways we might match our writing with the theoretical challenges going on in the world. We still run a little scared of poetry and emotion, a little scared of making ourselves visible. As Ann Oakley demonstrated, research projects often grow out of real life dramas.[8] When we analyse our own practices, our own lives, we can learn how to look at history anew, to imagine things we might also have experienced in another time, as other selves. Within the historical narrative (not just the book's introduction) experience can be the beginning point of questions. Potentially understanding her or his lived experience better, the writer understands the emotions of history better. While the inclusion of personal experience is no egalitarian solution, in losing full disguise, authors share their common humanity with their historical subjects and their readers.[9]

I was hoping to practice reflexivity as a conduit, as a device which would be part of my historical practice, not as a means of launching into autobiography itself. In part, it was also a reaction to what Aboriginal historians had been saying to us for some time: 'Why don't you explore your own histories? Why are you talking so much about ours?' My paper started with a dramatic retelling of the birth of my first daughter. *Performances* had become an empowering text, but somehow getting up in front of an AHA audience and telling such a recent and intimate story seemed at the time a very risk-taking exposure. Its woman-centredness made it not much like *Performances* at all. I turned from my daughter's birth to a call for a story of women's experiences of childbirth for the coming Centenary of Australian Federation in 2001. I had a 'fire in the belly' about this project which will become a Museum exhibition at the Powerhouse. Reflexively speaking, the history of birth also became a way of doing something I wouldn't be doing any more in real life. This new historical journey was a way of coming to terms with that.

Australian Historical Association conferences require earnest papers with clever arguments; at this one, in 1996, some elders were eloquent, poetic, and funny, though they followed the rules of argument and scholarly detachment. The AHA was a broad church, and it nicely reflected the values of the profession. Reflexivity was of course permitted in special venues where historians were asked to reflect upon their careers. It was mainly permitted for old retired scholars who spent their time on autobiography, considered a different genre, but one several historians enjoyed. But generally, the personal only entered as a joking aside, as part of a toastmaster's repertoire; it was done, then finished.

While self-conscious about the idea of exposing a personal story of extreme physical, mental and emotional vulnerability, the challenge was also exhilarating. I had doubts too, wondering whether my public exposure of the intimate merely followed the popular craze for television revelation, *à la* Oprah Winfrey and the other highly successful American talkshows of the time. Was I just indulging in some therapeutic narrative? Australian humour says you should all feel just as ridiculous as me, only there's a plotline around me doing some pretty amazing stuff. Yeah, giving birth. Although told with self-deprecating honesty, perhaps my birth story *was* a chance to share a bit of self-aggrandisement; I experienced it as a happily heroic narrative, but one in which my character paradoxically enjoyed only incidental control.

Like a naughty schoolgirl, I found defying the norms at an AHA conference a fun idea. The style of the childbirth story was experiential rather than a graphically medical perspective. While I enjoyed giving the paper, it probably had no impact whatever on historians' attitudes to reflexivity. I had just *done* it. Although self-consciously making a kind of in-your-face statement, I hadn't argued about it or theorised it. In conclusion I discussed my reflections upon the relationship between the 'self' and history, but mainly I was just demonstrating reflexivity. Now I wonder again about the difference between autobiography and history and where time comes in.

My imagined audience didn't turn up. There were younger historian colleagues, mainly women but several notable younger men. The male elders were all absent, choosing other sessions. Greg Dening was not at the conference at all. 'He may not be in Australia', people said.

An American historian friend disapproved, I could tell. Pat Grimshaw was concerned that my view was warped; it was nothing like her generation's experience of childbirth, I must study the demographics and statistics.

DEPARTURES

Fifty-one kilos or so of historian, embarking on comparative history, is transported across the date line. I'm in a Qantas Jumbo. The plane is full, but I am probably the only historian on it, the only one professionally excited about such a symbolic moment. I now wonder whether there is a place on the globe where we can cross the 'self-line', that divide between talking about general truth and personal truth, or between the self and history.

I was to give a seminar on inter-racial marriage in Queensland in the early 1900s at a prestigious United States University. In my Kensington home in Sydney, I had written much of it when I realised I was ignoring my new commitment to reflexivity. I must reflect upon my own ambivalent attitudes to marriage in the 1970s, which changed to embarking on it in 1988. I described how I felt during the wedding. My paper had to be sent in advance. The seminar organiser emailed me back at 10 pm US time. Trying not to be rude, she wanted to warn me that anyone conservative about such matters might attack the paper rather strongly, and cautioned me to consider leaving out the bit about my own marital history. I thought not. Although the paper was still too rough for my liking, I was happy with its risk-taking.

When I arrived there, she elaborated on why she'd advised me to change the paper. Certain elders weren't ready for this kind of thing yet, she said protectively. They'd obsess about it. It was not history to them, maybe the end of it. Some were very distinguished and set in their ways. I got an impression that these people, whose names I didn't know, were not only highly regarded, but untouchable in their prestige and achievement. She tried to brief me about who they were, and warned me of the kind of trouble I could face. To fill in time before the paper, I visited the bookshop, to see row upon row of books by some of the seminar participants about whom I'd just been briefed. Some contained a lot of tabulated data.

As the seminar audience had plenty of time to read in advance, I only had to provide a brief introduction. At the outset I made some joking observations about my journey to the United States, which didn't seem to go over that well. A leading feminist historian asked the first question, which began surprisingly: 'I guess I would locate myself as a fairly conservative historian, but I wondered about whether there would be different strategies by which to include a reflexive strand. You could explore how you went about the historical research and the process of history-writing more reflexively.' And she provided many clever directions. I'd met this historian in Sydney, and she was acting out of friendship and the loyalty of another fellow feminist historian. She later told me this ploy was to 'locate herself strategically' so that the whole discussion did not needlessly focus on 'the problem' of reflexivity. The astuteness of her political game impressed—the deceptive woman of her leisuretime cowgirl jacket and Akubra hat was in serious mode, heading 'them' off at the grand corral. As she was probably seen by many historians as radical and even postmodernist, with her recent interest in street culture as opposed to her earlier Marxist-inspired analyses of class and work relations, she had instantaneously redefined the ground of historical conservatism. After a rich and diverse discussion, the chair intervened by saying that he didn't see how the reflexive bit about my own marriage assisted the paper and that perhaps it would have been a stronger paper without it. What, if anything, had it achieved? I said its virtue was that we were having this interesting discussion.

The seminar was outstandingly rich, thoughtful, well-informed and helpful. But it was one of the younger, theoretically adventurous, scholars who was more agitated than anyone else. From his dark-skinned perspective, and of African-American politics and history, he said the fact that I'd gone steady with a boy of Asian descent was hardly much of a foray into mixed marriage. How could I personally relate to the topic with such minimal, possibly irrelevant, experience? He had been married and had a child to a white woman. I wasn't to know this then, but it was obvious he spoke from some personal engagement with, as well as an awareness of, the wider politics of the topic. In the United States, as elsewhere, 'black' meant something quite different from Asian.

Afterwards, the historian elder said I was a clever interlocutor, a word I cannot pronounce, which is the best kind of compliment, and I was honoured that she took my work seriously. I didn't mind ruffling some feathers, and was pleased with the way I'd risen to the challenging questions of an audience who had accorded the paper a very close and careful reading. When I gave a similar paper at New York University, people shared comparative examples from far afield countries like Russia, and remarked on the great policy contrasts between Australia and the US. Only afterwards did a student tell me about her own thesis on race, where she was to explore her personal experience of inter-marriage. For her, it would be an important intellectual and personal journey and she'd enjoyed hearing me articulate questions of inter-marriage, history-writing and re-flexivity. Although she had not yet commenced her postgraduate studies, I knew her voice was essentially more 'author-ised' than my own.

A day or two after this paper, my friend took me to the home of her colleagues, a couple who'd recently found each other. It was an elegant Baltimore home, with light and space, and posters evoking art and the political. They shared a richly cultured exist-ence, surrounded by great books everywhere. The talk was about their move, a teenage son, their cat and academic gossip. *Performances* sat on the coffee table. They loved it.

So it wasn't the reflexivity that was the problem. It was the substance and relevance of the reflexivity. It is only years later that I can see the discomfort was not merely at 'the new'. It was at some boundary-pushing that hadn't worked. The lesson I have now learnt is that only if one's personal experience can truly inform the subject matter at hand, metaphorically or experientially, is it worthy of inclusion. In that paper on marriage, the reflexive section had focussed on my attitude to weddings, my reaction at the moments of the wedding, whereas my paper had been about state surveillance. There was no state surveillance involved in my wedding plans, so I couldn't say much on that issue. While my fiance was a Pakeha New Zealander, we just had to register at a police station and contact a marriage celebrant in Alice Springs. Some kind of reciprocal national arrangement meant there were no citizenship problems or obstacles of any kind. My 1970s ambivalence to marriage was quite irrelevant to the people I was studying who struggled to marry in frontier Queensland during the 1900s. This section of the paper, although occurring somewhere in the middle, functioned as an atoll, insufficiently related to its historical surroundings, and where connections were made, the bands were at snapping point.

Reflexive insights must involve what you truly know. And they must truly relate to the topic under study, or they are a mere distraction, flotsam better left to float out to sea. The reflexive in history, therefore, should be closely related to the process, or it should open avenues by which the subject matter can be understood in fresh ways. Reflexivity, like other historical tools and equipment, must be functional; it must work.

THE RESEARCH ADVENTURE

As well as self-reflexivity, do we have a special obligation to share the journey of scholarship, to be reflexive about the research and writing process? Should we start our chapters by describing our office surroundings, or the sites of our researches? Do our introductory remarks take the reader to the archives, describing the desks and chairs, the demeanour of the staff, the excitement and distractions of the fellow researchers, the unfolding personal histories or research stories that make fascinating eavesdropping? What thoughts float through the researcher's mind as they reshape themselves, remake themselves via the process of amazing discoveries?

As performers we must draw a crowd, and it's worth noting that the crowd may have different demands. Some may want to learn about 'history'; they may not want to share the trip with you, but rather want to get directly to destination B. They may consider a historian's concern with 'self' in a derogatory fashion, as our cultural heritage often uses 'self' words as demeaning, for example 'self-absorbed', 'selfish'. Other readers, however, may be keenly interested to share your travels.

Field work, oral history-collecting and going to sites where histories happened offers its own rich stories, those of conflicts and misunderstandings, boredoms, awakenings and disappointments and, perhaps more than anything, the naïve researcher's misguided insights. The frustrations, the weeds encountered, can sometimes blossom into something grand. From my Northern Territory field work from 1978 and 1979, I have diaries which recount aspects of the process of gathering oral history on northern cattle stations. Between their cardboard covers I found a place to report to my doctoral supervisor, John Hirst, and to reflect to myself about my research experiences. For many years, they have sat on shelves with only other books for company. Once I opened them, found an embarrassing phrase or two, and closed them again. The embarrassment came because I saw myself exposed as a white colonising woman. Hardly surprising, but words can reveal something you were desperately trying to ignore at the time. Leave them in a closed book. If I open these old field notes again, I will try another page, for I would like something more romantic, some wet heat or orange dust, to fly out and settle on my clothing.

Historians' journeys into the past both bring them away from and towards their self. Each project presents opportunities to struggle not only with distant others, but with old and new selves in a process of recreation. Each project has a different 'self-line' and the trick is to find out where it is. You may or may not want to tell that parallel story of your intellectual travels, or reveal your historians' disguise. You may want to use your voice only in that traditional 'beginning space', or somewhere else. Find out for yourself whether it will lead to new vistas, unexpected connections, or disjunctions and unresolved, curiously 'life-like', endings.

In 1998, I met up with Greg Dening again at the Centre for Cross-Cultural Research at the Australian National University. I picture us talking on the concrete stairs above the Lower Ground Floor of the A.D. Hope Building, a sun-dappled, leafy outdoor space, each of us heading in different directions. I told him I'd written a letter to him, but hadn't sent it. He said he'd like to see the letter. I told him: 'It wasn't good enough. It didn't match your prose.' His retort: 'Doesn't matter, just send it.' I never did.

ENDNOTES

1   P. Grimshaw *et al.*, *Creating a Nation*, McPhee Gribble/Penguin, Ringwood, 1994, had explored reproductive and birth metaphors. The birth-giving of two Aboriginal women in early Port Jackson had operated as a framing metaphor for that chapter, and, because of its placement, it was said to do so for the book as a whole.

2   G. Dening, *Performances*, Melbourne University Press, Melbourne, 1996. To avoid a narrative approach which is too teleological, I wish to inform the reader in this behind-the-curtains fashion that *Performances* was not my first encounter with Dening's histories. It did, however, function as a significant turning point, stimulating my interest in issues of historical style and issues of reflexivity. Nor was Dening's work my first encounter with the riches of the 'ethnographic school of history'; I had also been a doctoral student at La Trobe University, with senior historians including Rhys Isaacs and Inga Clendinnen. Sometime earlier I was asked to present a paper on Birthplaces at a Museum of Sydney Conference, 'Exchanges', organised by Ross Gibson. Here I not only heard Greg Dening give an amazing paper about

ocean navigation, science and the sky, which subtly turned its lens onto big history reflections upon the cosmos; at question time he provided a mini-exposition on the minutiae of an early popular drama of Captain Cook. My paper was about birthplaces of Aboriginal and convict women. I'd also heard Greg Dening speak of Bligh's bad language at a conference at the University of Sydney. This I was not sure about, for it seemed stilted. This, in contrast to his Exchanges address, was wildly lateral and free in conception.

3   G. Dening, 'Let My Curiosity Have its Little Day', *Australian Book Review*, no. 180, 1996, pp. 38, 40.

4   The best-known works by these authors are P. Limerick, *The Legacy of Conquest: The Unbroken Past of the American West*, Norton, New York, 1987, and R. White, *The Middle Ground: Indians, Empires and Republics in the Great Lakes Region 1650–1815*, Cambridge University Press, New York, 1991.

5   Dening, *Performances*, p. 3, refers only to 'self-conceit' and the point does not seem to be made in as extreme a form as I implied in the letter. However, it emerges at the end of the book, in 'Soliloquy in San Giacomo': 'It is an arrogance and sometimes a bore to begin with oneself. But I do not know where else to begin, where else to find the same, where else to find the different' (p. 272).

6   Here I was referring to my reading of Clifford Geertz, *The Interpretation of Cultures*, Basic Books, Inc., New York, 1973, and *After the Fact: Two Countries, Four Decades, One Anthropologist*, Harvard University Press, Cambridge, Mass., 1995. Although I thoroughly enjoyed and was inspired by his work, I wondered where we would go from there, that is, if the endpoint was that scholars could only be able to reflect upon ourselves. More recently, Aboriginal historians and other authors have been calling upon white Australians to do just that, to learn their own family histories, about their own distant roots, rather than prying into Aboriginal history.

7   These questions followed the draft letter. I don't think I intended to integrate them in text, I was just 'jotting' down thoughts.

8   A. Oakley, *Becoming a Mother*, Martin Robinson, Oxford, 1979, p. 20 and *passim*.

9   'Births of a Nation', AHA Paper, 1996. I explored the issue of 'selves in history' more thoroughly, and via reflecting upon my teenage diaries, in an article entitled 'The Female Eunuch in the Suburbs: Reflections upon Adolescence, Autobiography, and History-Writing', *Journal of Popular Culture*, vol. 33, no. 1, 1999, pp. 177–90. For a philosophical analysis, see G. Lloyd, *Being in Time: Selves and Narrators in Philosophy and Literature*, Routledge, London and New York, 1993.

CHAPTER 8

WRITING PLACE

Deborah Bird Rose

I am speaking from my own efforts at writing place. I hope not to be too abstract, because I want to engage with an experiential process: how my research with Aboriginal people caused me to write about place, and how writing place changed the way I write and think. Aboriginal people in many parts of Australia have taught me to consider that country is sentient. Place is one kind of embodiment of being, and the encounters of living things happen in places. Different cultures, different actions: different traces. Aboriginal cultures link time and place in a way that is neither geometric nor disembodied. There is a kind of contemporaneous time, the time of living things, that unfolds in real and located (not geometric or imagined) places. As well there is the accumulation of history/memory in place. Place become complex in its specific gravity: it is and refers to itself, and it holds and refers to relationships. Its very self, while wondrously dense, is also immensely vulnerable, because the ongoing life of the place happens through the actions and memories of ephemeral living beings.

In my work I have sought to communicate the vitality of the living world in its multiplicity of places. I seek to retain in my writing the life and the sense of place, the vulnerabilities of relationships, and the passion with which living things encounter each other in place.

PROMISES/PROBLEMS

If an author takes a place-centred approach to research and writing he or she destabilises many of the conventional concepts of twentieth-century western knowledge. This destabilisation is one of the great promises of writing place. It may be useful, therefore, to say why I think destabilising conventional concepts is a good thing to do. The main instrumental reason is that the conventions of the dominant western system of knowledge are taking us deeper and deeper into the ecological and social crises we face today. Destabilising this system is critical to finding ways of thinking and acting that may help us start to face these crises. I want to face crisis and work with it; I hope not to reproduce and aggravate it. A second reason to put positive value on destabilisation is that we are now in a period of rapid social change; global geography is shrinking and becoming ever more connected. Our task as scholars, as I see it, is to pay serious and critical attention to the world *as it is becoming*, and such attention will necessarily require us to destabilise our given knowledge. Knowledge that looks for structure and permanence must be destabilised in favour of theories of knowledge that work with relationships and motion. Place provides exactly a nexus of analysis that calls for study of relationships and motion.

When I use the term 'conventional' here and throughout my chapter, I am referring to academic disciplines as they have existed for much of this century, and using anthropology and history as two prominent examples. I will look briefly at how concepts of social group and concepts of time are challenged by place, but in doing so I do not mean to suggest that these are the only concepts which are challenged by place.

In the discipline of anthropology, social groups have been the focus of analysis for almost all of the twentieth century. The community was a social group that had a geographical location (localised or dispersed), but was defined by social and cultural criteria, many of which have been the subject of on-going debates. In these debates communities, tribes, bands, neighbourhoods, whatever, have all been defined, delimited, perhaps invented, probably deformed; most often they were abstracted from the places and conductivities in which they were embedded. (The move toward cultural ecology is an interesting exception to this generalisation.)

Similarly, in history, the concept of the nation or some community within the nation has been one of the prominent organising configurations. A nation has a geographical location; territory is a key criterion of nationhood. None the less, the only way we can understand so many decades of Australian histories that said little or nothing about Aboriginal people is if we understand the nation as a social event over and above its territorial location. Aborigines have been here the whole time, but they figured only marginally (if at all) in scholarship for long periods. Nations, like communities, can be represented as bounded social groups, and one can study the group without having to consider other people who occupy exactly the same time and place. In contrast to communities and nations, a place-centred study will not let you ignore the people who are there. You will be unable to make sense of a place if you leave out whole groups of peoples or whole sets of processes. A place-centred study is going to be much more holistic than conventional topics of study; place does not pick and choose, the way scholars so often do.

When we look at time we see similar destabilisation. Anthropologists have drawn on western time concepts in their construction of others, as Johannes Fabian shows so eloquently in his study, *Time and the Other*.[1] Simultaneously, however, anthropologists have tended to suppress questions of time within the locus of their study. Many anthropologists examined social groups as if they were outside of time (representing them in an ahistorical present), or as if they were simply a window to an earlier time. The ruthlessness of this latter approach can hardly be overestimated. To value people for the perspective their lives can bring to bear on one's own questions, and for the documentation of a 'time' that is passing, can be callous in the extreme. A clear and relatively recent example is located in A.P. Elkin's article 'Before it is Too Late' (written about the purpose of the Australian Institute of Aboriginal Studies[2]):

> 'Before it is too late' has been a recurrent challenge to research in Australian Aboriginal Anthropology. Faced by the sure and certain dying out of tribes and by the even quicker breakdown of their culture, George Taplin … [and numerous others] recognised and responded to the challenge. With the help of correspondents near and far, they observed, gleaned and garnered what and where they could … As with search in the mineral and oil fields, so, too, the Institute [of Aboriginal Studies] is observing, surveying, probing, sounding, drilling and extracting. The dividends will be high, though probably not in every project. Some fields are poor.[3]

Historians, in contrast, cannot ignore time, but they have been remarkably uncritical of their own use of time concepts. Many twentieth-century histories have been organised around chronologies that impose an external frame of bounded units onto flows of events and social relations that are heterogeneous, differentially configured across space, interpenetrating and (often) culturally disjunctive. The imposition of chronology calls for some measure of uniformity, and thus of suppression or elision of events that disrupt the chrono-story. Thus, for example, Vance Palmer's study of the quickening literary life in Australia during the decade of the 1890s makes no mention of the literary output of Constable Willshire, whose *Land of the Dawning, Being Facts Gleaned from Cannibals in the Australian Stone Age* was published in this decade.[4] During the 1890s Constable Willshire was sent to the Victoria River district in what is now the Northern Territory (then part of South Australia) to 'settle the natives'. His settlement tactics were about as rough as they could be: massacre, dispersal, capture, sexual terror, and torture. His work was not unique; he employed all the elements of terror that were used elsewhere in Australia to dispossess indigenous people and secure the land for Euro-Australian settlers, or, more accurately, to secure the land for their livestock. And yet, here in the Victoria River district, there were those who were dissatisfied with Willshire's methods. A contributor to the *Northern Territory Times* put the case:

There will never be much done towards steadying the Victoria blacks until sufficient police are sent out there, or, in default of that, until the squatters are given carte blanche to disperse the enemy in the old-fashioned pioneering, survival-of-the-fittest way.[5]

Vance Palmer writes that in this decade the legend that 'the dumb continent, silent for aeons, began to find voice' was nurtured.[6] A focus on place requires us to look again at this presumption. Not only are Aboriginal people's voices silenced for all time in Palmer's encompassing sentence, but so too are the voices of those who actually were killing and otherwise silencing Aboriginal people.[7] Constable Willshire distances himself from his own violence by displacing it onto his weapons, and describes events of extreme brutality in the language of the sublime. The various speech moments in this famous passage make a mockery of the idea of a dumb and silent continent: 'It's no use mincing matters—the Martini-Henry carbines at this critical moment were talking English in the silent majesty of those great eternal rocks.'[8]

Another aspect of scholars' imposition of Euro-Australian time concepts is the organisation of events within a temporal construct in which events overcome and transform earlier events. This time frame depends on disjunctures, so that any given time can be differentiated from the past, and is (or is about to be) superseded—by new eras, new centuries, new frontiers. This progress-oriented time construct enables moral boundaries at least as readily as it enables temporal ones. We know this kind of thinking best today through the words of politicians who exhort us to forget the past. They point us towards the future, while simultaneously they are disabling the systems that have existed to enable injustices of the past to be overcome. The call to forget the past is accompanied by practices that perpetuate the past, and the link between the two is hidden beneath an illusion of discontinuity generated in the proposition that the past is finished.[9]

In sum, when you start to do a place-centred study, you find that conventional notions of community or other bounded social groups do not work very well; you find that you cannot predetermine questions of time; and you may find that conventional notions of time do not work very well. Place requires you to be intercultural, inter-temporal, open-minded to the imperatives of the lives that are lived there. If you are going to do a place-centred study, you have to destabilise a lot of boundaries and a lot of conventions. You thus go against the grain of established power as well as established thinking.

PERILS

This brings me to the first of two perils that I want to talk about. It is one thing to challenge yourself, and you should always do that. It is another thing to challenge those around you, many of whom may not want to be challenged. I will speak from personal experience.

My book, *Hidden Histories*, was written quite directly as reciprocity to the people of the main communities in which I had done my anthropological research.[10] I did not think that my ethnography, *Dingo Makes Us Human*, was going to be a great contribution to my Aboriginal teachers, mostly because it concerned a lot of things that they took for granted. However, they did not take for granted the stories of their own past. They wanted a lot of these stories published: for white Australians who didn't know, for Americans and others who might want to know, and for their own future generations who, they feared, might forget.

One of the things I hoped to accomplish in this book was a complex weaving of voices and subject positions. I wanted to keep my own subject position dialogical and open-ended, and I had two reasons for this: one is that this is, I believe, the most ethically appropriate position for a scholar who conducts research with human beings. The second reason concerns the nature of the time, place and intercultural relations I was dealing with. I was writing out of the North Australian frontier, and it seems to me that one of the outstanding features of frontiers is the gap between an event and one's ability to comprehend it. The Victoria River district was a long and violent frontier, in many ways it still is. I did not want to position myself on an intellectual height where all was made comprehensible. I cannot comprehend that violence, and neither can you. We show respect for the dead as well as for the survivors, and for the enormity of their experience, by refusing to provide resolution in the sense of settling the meaning of the experience. I wanted to communicate the non-resolvable quality of many of the events about which people told me, and I believe that I could do that best from a position of open-ended dialogue.

Now, I also wanted to communicate the fact that there was a logic that informed Aboriginal people's stories. It was not a logic of time or resolution, nor for the most part about how things get superseded. Rather it was a logic of place. People told stories that they had a right to tell because they happened in their own country or country to which they had rights. Often these were stories that had happened to their forebears. The place, the person and the story: all were part of the place-centred logic that made that story memorable, and tellable.

I thought hard about how to communicate it. This logic is obviously a crucial point, and in the end I decided against presenting a theoretical analysis of place in Aboriginal concepts of story and history. I felt that to do that would subvert my dialogical subject position; it just did not seem appropriate to the ethical foundations of this book for me to engage in my own little tap dance about place and story. The point had to be made, and could most ethically be made in respect of every speaker, so I decided to make it structurally. Every story would be accompanied by a map showing exactly where the place was. Places would not be abstract names, but would be actual locations. Every story and map would be accompanied by a photo that showed the story-teller or one of his or her countrymen. Story-tellers would not be just names or voices, but would have faces and places. And most stories would also be accompanied by a photo that showed the place, either historically or contemporaneously, or some aspect of the event that was being told about. This required a complex structure, and in order for the reader to get the sense of it all in the text presented to the publisher, I indicated exactly where I thought these photos and maps would have to go.

I do not know if my structural strategy would have successfully communicated all that I hoped for it, and I guess I will never know, because in the process of publication my whole structure was unmade, jumbled up, and, in effect, ruined. The book was raced off to the printer before I saw the page proofs. One minute I was waiting for the page proofs and still arguing about an index, the next minute I had a copy of the book in my hand.

I couldn't begin to tell you how traumatic this was. Later the book won a prize, and that helped overcome my anguish to some degree. The prize had a cash award, and that money paid the lawyer who I had had to employ in order simply to press the publisher to include an *errata* so that interested readers could make some sense of it.

My point is that when you stretch yourself, you are asking others to stretch themselves too. One of the perils of working beyond the established tried and true is that you carry a huge burden of trying to ensure that your work lives up to its potential. There will be people who don't understand its potential and who try to pull it back into established norms. There will be people who don't understand its potential and therefore don't take it seriously.

If you choose to work at the edges your strength rests with the people who are also at the edge. If you are working on the edge, you know that it is the most interesting place to be. Cherishing the people with whom you share this cutting edge zone is a very important way of affirming your commitment to certain kinds of disruptive and enabling knowledge.

Another peril that relates to place is this: almost anything that is written in Australia today that says anything about Aboriginal people has the potential to end up in court as part of a native title case. (This is also true of some non-place-centred studies.) You have a non-negotiable ethical obligation to be extremely accurate in your writing on these matters. Flights of imagination, judiciously managed, can contribute a great deal to scholarship, but they have no place in pronouncements on matters concerning other people's lives. One cannot predict how one's words will be used, and for that reason one has a deep ethical obligation to be accurate and restrained. I am not in any way advocating that you refrain from working with Aboriginal people, or that you refrain from making statements about Aboriginal people. We need good histories, good cultural accounts, the more the better. Nor am I suggesting that scholarship should be deflected away from tough issues. Rigorous scholarship is more necessary now than perhaps ever before. The possibility of hostile scrutiny in court challenges us to be doubly or triply clear, concise and consistent with the evidence. You should know that, if required, you can get into the witness box with confidence that your words say exactly what you mean, that your meaning does not exceed the limits of the evidence, and that your meaning does not foreclose on the future which is, we should all remember, unknown.

POSSIBILITIES

There are more cheerful topics. I will discuss a few segments from my book *Country of the Heart: An Indigenous Australian Homeland*.[11] The book is a photo-essay. It aims to communicate a portrait of the relationship between an Aboriginal group of people and their land. The group is called the MakMak clan, or clan of the white breasted sea eagle. This study is place-centred, and also people-centred, and most specifically it is centred on the relationships between people and place. In this Aboriginal context, the relationships between people and place consist of connections and communications. This means that I am treating place as a conscious entity with agency.

You see, if I take my MakMak teachers seriously, and I do, then, like them, I have to start engaging with a sentient landscape. Such an approach destabilises the whole system of subject-object dichotomies on which the conventional western knowledge system depends, so it is perhaps not surprising that it encounters a measure of backlash. In this book I seek to communicate something of the quality of relationships between and among specific embodied people, animals, plants and places. These relationships are sustained by all the senses, and by memory and other intellectual work. They are emotional, experienced right down in the gut, and they are intellectual: talked about, narrated, sung, laughed over. And they are emplaced, located not on a Cartesian grid, but embodied in the place.

In *Country of the Heart* I am working with four strands of narrative: there is my own textual strand, the textual strand of the Aboriginal countrymen with whom I am co-authoring this work, the visual strand produced by Sharon D'Amico, a professional eco-photographer, and the structure of the book itself which, I believe, constitutes a narrative strand in itself.

I will share with you the opening sequence. The first question, of course, is how to get readers into the place, in what attitude, and with what perspectives. I wanted to use this sequence to allude to and at the same time to subvert the dominant colonising gaze. I have chosen to start with the elevated gaze described so well by Simon Ryan in his book, *The Cartographic Eye*.[12] I unsettle this gaze; in the first instance I set you above but will not let you look down. Your gaze is elevated, but not totalising, and the text works with this position. I bring you in as a tourist, and in this opening sequence I mimic explorer writing (which is itself also mimicked or reflected in tourist promotion writing).

> Fly to Darwin in the Northern Territory of Australia, and rent a four wheel drive vehicle. Drive south-west to Litchfield National Park, going through the little bush town of Batchelor. As you near the park you leave the flat scrub of the Darwin hinterland and begin to climb the Table Top Range. There comes a moment when you cross the water-shed and catch a glimpse of the enormous western sky. The traces of smoke will tell you that there is land over there, and that the country is being fired. The dense manner in which the light hangs in the air on the far horizon will tell you that the sea is there beyond. You feel transfixed, and yet, nothing in these densities and opacities of light, air, water, and fire tells you of the violence and the love that are connected to this place.
>
> You are seeing the sky that rests over one of the most contested areas in Australia.

From here I let readers look down at the ground, and, through a series of aerial shots and large-scale landscape photos, I bring them to the hill country where the rivers start up. From there we follow the rivers to the floodplains: 'these are northern rivers, huge in the wet season, smaller in the dry, roaring down off the hills and meandering across the plains.' Out on the floodplains swamps and billabongs hold the water. Here we will see a small rainforest, and we go inside to look at it. Once inside the jungle we see a place within the spring where the water actually bubbles up out of the ground. The Aboriginal traditional owners of this country call this the 'eye'—the 'eye' of the spring.

So I bring you from the sky down to the ground. I use the fluidity of water to accomplish this motion, and bring you down almost into the ground. From the elevated eye of the explorer, who imagines himself to be encompassing all that he sees, I bring you face to face with another eye. This eye is part of the place, and it is looking back at you.

Here I pause to tell you:

> There are 'eyes' all over this country; this is a place where living things take notice of each other. People travel across the land, and they watch, observe, remember, think about, and tell stories. Other living things—birds, Dreamings, ordinary animals—they all watch, observe, think, and tell stories. This place is sentient.

And from there the book opens out into a sentient and intersubjective world. The next photo you see is (finally) a person. The person is one of the senior traditional owners, Kathy Deveraux. The text voice that accompanies this photo is hers:

IT'S LIKE THE SPIDER:
A LOT OF THINGS TIE IN TOGETHER,
SO WHEN YOU ASK ONE THING
YOU GET A WHOLE BIG HISTORY.

Place-centred stories tie in associatively around the place. One could imagine stories strung together by time, or by focus on a central character, or by the logic of cause and effect as construed in western reason. Aboriginal place-centred stories are most regularly strung together by sites and tracks, by memories, permanencies and linked contingencies, as well as by a way of life that keeps people returning to places and telling stories for places.

Throughout the book the analysis requires linking place with time. I try to hold to a place-oriented perspective as I do this. If one were to take a time-oriented view of this place, at least as time is conventionally understood in the western academy, one might seek to sort out layers of events. One might take an archaeological approach and, through digging into meaning, one would find differences (technological, ecological, perhaps even ontological), and one would sort those differences into a sequence. If you look at a lot of texts and notice how many of them begin with sacred origins, then move to secular sequences, beginning with the earliest and ending with the most recent, you will see a time-oriented approach at work. A place-oriented approach does not require any particular notion of time; we do not see layers so much as webs. A great deal of what can be thought of as sequence is actually located right there on the ground. People walk across, live with it, and interact with it. The 'past' both is and is not past. Present in the land, interactive in memory, and alive to the happenings of the present, the so-called past lives in the present in the most vivid ways. And so I have written:

> Webs are connections, and the heart of these connections is the concept of the return. Aboriginal peoples move from place to place, from waterhole to waterhole, called by the seasons, the resources, the global economy, the Dreaming tracks, and the Law. Their movement is predicated upon their return. The tracks are recursive, and the country holds the signs which constitute the evidence of their presence, along with the evidence of the presence of Dreamings and of previous generations of people, as well as many non-human events.

A brief look at one particular billabong makes this point. This is a Dreaming place for the Rainbow Snake. He tried to steal the fire, and carry it away across the floodplains to the sea. He went this way and that, twisting across the land trying to get to the sea, and when he failed he came back and died right here. The evidence of his activities across the floodplains and here at this billabong is completely explicit: it can be seen in the sandy bottom of the billabong, the great meanders of the rivers, and the old river beds that no longer carry water.

At this same billabong one sees graded fence lines where paddocks have been enclosed; one sees a little hill where unexplained lights appear from time to time. There is a ridge where people lived only a few years ago, old river beds, old bull-catching camps, the traces of a bush fire from a few years ago, the encroaching *mimosa pigra*, a noxious weed that will destroy the country if it cannot be stopped. There is a site where there used to be a jungle. All of this is here and visible (except the vanished jungle). When the traditional owners of this place interact with it they bring all this knowledge and memory to bear. They know of the former jungle because their forebears told them so, and nearby are the graves of some of the old people. Memory, or history, lies in the land, and is carried through stories.

I will conclude with a few words about the senses. Every study has its own imperatives. This study has demanded of me a much greater engagement with all the senses than I have hitherto accomplished. I have sought to communicate that engagement in many of my own words. The emphasis on the full sensorium is not my invention: my Aboriginal teachers engage with country this way, and if one is to learn to understand the communicative dimension of the relationships between people and country this is how one has to pay attention.

> 'You don't stay away for very long, do you?' [Kathy said to her mother Nancy Daiyi. Nancy replied:]
>
> 'No. I can never stay too long. Otherwise I will get properly homesick. I mean really sick. I miss the smell and the sound of the swamp and all the activities and characteristics of the animals. I can picture them. My senses taste the sweet smell of the [floating grass] on the billabongs when it gets burnt and starts shooting again. The fat from our turtle, geese and barramundi is not the same anywhere else in the world.'[13]

BY WAY OF A CONCLUSION

Many authors suggest that we distinguish space—the abstract, geometric and plot-table—from place. Place is the domain of the real, a nexus of space/time, a site with specific presence and with a history. Whether it is a swamp or a high rise, an urban jungle or a tropical rainforest, place is a nexus of living things. People's actions become, and are formed by, the locale. Two streams of western thought work to bolster this distinction. Science, as David Abram (like others) notes, privileges a sensible field in abstraction from sensory experience.[14] Concurrent with this thinking about science, we also have an interesting literature about reading, and the disembodiment of the eye.[15] I would like to suggest that as science is to sensorial experience, so reading is to knowing, and space is to place. Reading potentially detaches the eye from the body, just as space potentially detaches the body from the world. If reading reduces the sensorium to the purely/merely visual, mapping flattens and silences the land as Paul Carter demonstrates so brilliantly.[16] The body is displaced to become an appendage to the eye; the living world is displaced to become an appendage to the text/map/GIS. In the extreme, reading/mapping could be thought to struggle toward relationship between a disembodied eye and a displaced world.

These dis-placements, or perhaps more properly mis-placements, were key moves in the development of the dominant western knowledge system. An emphasis on place, on real place as experienced by people whose lives are embedded in those places, thus destabilises this knowledge system. Such an emphasis calls on researchers to open themselves methodologically to the fullest possible sensuous engagement. It calls researchers into ethical engagements with place and people: there is no unconnected relationship to place. Place-oriented research calls for writing that seeks to do justice, ethically and methodologically, to the richness of time, human endeavour, and the multiplicities of living things whose tracks cross a given place. As well, it asks one to find ways seriously to engage with non-human endeavour, to enlarge one's concept of agency, and to write about matters that are often disregarded within the academy.

The word 'love' comes to mind. Love is so central to place that it shimmers on the horizons of much of our writing. How we would bring love into the heart of writing place I do not exactly know. For ethical reasons and for the future of scholarship and the future of places, I believe that we must do so.

ENDNOTES

1   J. Fabian, *Time and the Other: How Anthropology Makes its Object*, Columbia University Press, New York, 1983.

2   Now known as the Australian Institute of Aboriginal and Torres Strait Islander Studies.

3   A.P. Elkin, 'Before it is Too Late', in R. Berndt (ed.), *Australian Aboriginal Anthropology*, AIAS and University of Western Australia Press, Nedlands, 1970, p. 19.

4   W. Willshire, *The Land of the Dawning, Being Facts Gleaned From Cannibals in the Australian Stone Age*, W.K. Thomas Co, Adelaide, 1896.

5   *Northern Territory Times*, 10 June 1898.

6   V. Palmer, *The Legend of the Nineties*, Melbourne University Press, Melbourne, 1954, p. 9.

7   Discussed further in D. Rose, *Hidden Histories: Black Stories from Victoria River Downs, Humbert River and Wave Hill Stations*, Aboriginal Studies Press, Canberra, 1991, chapters 2 and 3.

8   Willshire, *The Land of the Dawning*, pp. 40–41.

9   D. Rose, 'Dark Times and Excluded Bodies in the Colonisation of Australia', in G. Gray and C. Winter (eds), *The Resurgence of Racism: Howard, Hanson and the Race Debate*, Monash Publications in History, Clayton, 1997, pp. 97–116.

10 The book was written in 1989.

11 This was published by Aboriginal Studies Press in 2002.

12 S. Ryan, *The Cartographic Eye*, Cambridge University Press, Cambridge, 1996.

13 K. Deveraux, 'Looking at Country From the Heart', in D. Rose and A. Clarke (eds), *Tracking Knowledge in North Australian Landscapes: Studies in Indigenous and Settler Ecological Knowledge Systems*, North Australian Research Unit, Darwin, 1998, p. 74.

14 D. Abram, *The Spell of the Sensuous: Perception and Language in a More-Than-Human World*, Vintage Books, New York, 1996, p. 66.

15 For example see M. Jay, *Downcast Eyes: The Denigration of Vision in Twentieth-Century French Thought*, University of California Press, Berkeley, 1993.

16 P. Carter, *The Lie of the Land*, Faber and Faber, London, 1996.

CHAPTER 9

THE PERSONAL IS HISTORICAL: WRITING ABOUT THE FREEDOM RIDE OF 1965

Ann Curthoys

Decades ago, when I was a History student, we were told never to use the pronoun 'I' when writing history. The aim was to write a third-person narrative in such a way that the narrator remained hidden, unknown, unimportant. This stricture is still passed on by some historians, as students are told to focus on the narrative, the story they have to tell, and to keep themselves well out of sight or hearing in the text. Yet the idea and practice of foregrounding the narrator, the story-teller, the historian, is rapidly gaining ground. We are learning to use the once-forbidden personal pronoun as a means of writing history, foregrounding the existence of interpretation in general, and our own interpretation in particular. By saying 'I', many argue, we are not aggrandising but rather relativising ourselves, drawing attention to the possibility of other views, interpretations, and ways of representing the past, to the limited and contingent nature of historical knowledge. By saying 'I', we leave the reader freer to judge and weigh up the historical narrative we have offered, and ourselves the space to admit to what we don't know, or cannot figure out.

Sometimes, though, the use of 'I' is important for a more direct reason — our own involvement in the events narrated. In the history I am writing of the Australian 'Freedom Ride' of 1965, the issue of narrational point of view becomes critical precisely because I was involved in the events myself. I am writing a history rather than an autobiography or memoir, partly because my own role in these events is relatively small, and partly because the project relies on extensive historical research into the wider historical context. In the early stages of the project I agonised quite a lot about the problems of the ex-participant as historian, concerned about issues of objectivity, believability, self-justification, and the like. If we are writing about events in which we were in some way involved, can we develop a truly historical perspective, or will there always be an element of self-justification, however unconscious? Even if there isn't, will our readers think there is? As the research has gone on, I have become less and less worried by these issues, as the sheer quantity of historical research — written and oral — takes over. But I still have the problem of form, of how to represent my own involvement while telling a much larger story. This is the problem I explore here.

The Australian 'Freedom Ride' took place in February 1965. At that time, a group of 30 university students from the University of Sydney, none of them Aboriginal except for their leading figure, Charles Perkins, travelled in a bus for two weeks around country towns in northern New South Wales, protesting against discrimination against Aboriginal people. It was consciously modelled on similar events in the southern United States, where especially in 1963 and 1964 both black and white civil rights campaigners had travelled in buses campaigning for basic civil rights for African Americans. The Australian students met with high levels of hostility from white townsfolk, massive media coverage, and stimulated widespread debate and concern over race relations in Australia. The significance of the event has since been debated, some seeing it as a turning point in the challenging of institutionalised racism in Australia, some seeing it as only a minor aspect of a much longer and larger protest movement for Aboriginal citizenship and civil rights, and some suggesting it held the struggle for Aboriginal full citizenship and civil rights back rather than pushed it forward.[1]

The Prologue to my book on these events may begin this way.

DAILY MIRROR, 20 FEBRUARY 1965. BY A SPECIAL REPORTER (GERALD STONE)

Sydney University students were attacked by a mob outside Moree swimming pool this afternoon. Many were punched and their clothes were spattered with ripe tomatoes and rotten fruit. A youth was arrested for punching a student and another for assaulting a Press photographer … As the students left the pool another two men were arrested … Earlier in the day, 10 students were thrown bodily from the entrance to the pool. The Mayor of Moree, Ald. W. Lloyd, helped to carry one of them. The students returned immediately and the baths manager then decided to close the pool. The students then decided to stay until the pool was reopened. A crowd of about 500 local residents became more hostile as the students' demonstration continued. The students were sitting in the shade at the baths entrance while the crowd, kept back by the police, were jammed together under the hot sun. About an hour before the demonstration ended at 5.30 pm the secretary of the students body, Mr Jim Spigelman, 19, of Maroubra, was assaulted. He was knocked to the ground after being hit in the stomach and on the chin by two youths … Another student, Mr John Butterworth, 20, of Turella, had his glasses smashed. Other students, including girls, complained they had been burnt with cigarette butts … The crowd jeered the students and tomatoes and rotten fruit were thrown at the students from behind the fence.

The Mayor and Deputy Mayor of Moree and two other aldermen then held an emergency meeting inside the pool with three student representatives, Mr Charles Perkins, Mr Spigelman and Miss Patricia Healy. Twenty minutes later, the Mayor, Alderman Lloyd, announced that two of the aldermen had agreed to sign a motion to rescind a resolution on the council book discriminating against aborigines. The resolution, passed in 1955, states that no person being an aboriginal or having an admixture of aboriginal blood should use, occupy or be present upon the area known as the bore baths or any associated facility …

The students then decided to leave the pool. The crowd by this time was becoming more violent. The police offered to escort the students through the back gate of the baths, but the students refused. The jeering rose to a deafening pitch as the students walked towards their bus at the front of the baths. Policemen and burly council workers tried to clear a path, but the crowd closed in. Some students were punched and others hit with rotten fruit. The side of the bus was also splattered with fruit as police escorted it out of town towards Inverell. Many cars followed the bus out of town …

GERALD STONE, INTERVIEW, 7 FEBRUARY 1994

Well, I suppose the perspective I'd give to that story was having come from the United States a couple of years before where the Freedom Rides were just beginning to become popular, or as a means of protest, and of course this was an Australian imitation, just the use of the word Freedom Ride was taken from the Americans at that time. I was amazed at how absolutely unsophisticated and pristine this political movement was … How young they were and what they were trying to do, it was very imitative, and I don't think they realised what they were tapping in the Australian psyche. In my mind a lot of the protest was not over the Aboriginal issue so much as some of these people were wearing beards and they were university students and there was a lot of antagonism that I remember from Moree …

They tried to get into the swimming pool, they were knocked back from the swimming pool. And everybody was very uncomfortable. I mean Australians are not exactly demonstrative people and country people are not out there to cause trouble. This was so new to everybody and nobody quite knew how to act, that the people that were trying to protect the Moree baths—I think the mayoral faction as I recall—and on the one hand they wanted to be firm and on the other they didn't want to cause trouble … But I still think at Moree that anything that happened there was more a reaction to the snotty-nosed university kids coming up from Sydney than any Aboriginal presence.

BILL LLOYD, FORMER MAYOR OF MOREE, INTERVIEWED BY ME, 5 APRIL 1991

I was at the State Emergency Service, talking to the Director, and some VIPs, when an urgent message came that there was trouble at the baths, and to come over. I left the function, and went straight over. You students were doing your passive resistance, obstructing entry to the baths, passive resistance came from South Africa I think. I had only a couple of council employees and the baths manager to help me. A huge crowd gathered. A lot of them were shearers, in town on a Saturday afternoon, a much bigger crowd than you would ever expect in Moree. The crowd grew, and it was very hostile to the students. There were Aborigines in the crowd, hostile to the students. It was a frightening awesome thing, a crowd out of control. I saw respected businessmen there, throwing tomatoes, eggs, and other things. I learnt then how awful a crowd out of control could be. The whole thing was getting out of hand …

The police refused to help, refused to remove the students from the baths, saying it was my responsibility and my problem. I rang two solicitors in town for advice, as I thought the police were obliged to help me, but the solicitors couldn't help. So I was on my own … I had to give all the instructions, the police wouldn't help. I found out later I shouldn't have had to do that, that the police should have helped. I arranged for the bus to be driven right up to the baths, and for the students to get on, with police assistance. We did it as quickly as possible, but there were still missiles thrown, and students were hit. The students got on the bus, and the police kept the crowd back from the bus. The police told the driver to get out of town, and escorted the bus out, so that no one would try and attack it. The police blocked all exits from the town, so no one could attack you students.

ANN CURTHOYS, DIARY ENTRY 20 FEBRUARY 1965

We went on to Moree, arriving at about 12.30 pm. We went straight to Thompson's Row, where the 'town' aborigines live. We found that that morning the aboriginal children there had been given swimming club tickets which meant that they could enter the baths at any time. The children from Bingara Rd and the Mission had not got these tickets, and were refused entry.

The Thompson's Row people obviously felt little or no sympathy for the other aborigines and were not prepared to fight for them. A case of 'divide and rule' as most of us soon realised. Then we went to the Mission. Bill refused to drive the bus onto the mission, so Charlie and Beth went … The manager wouldn't let them stay and so they only had time to ask about 4 or 5 of the kids to come along. Sue and Chris went in Bob Brown's car to get some kids from the Bingara Rd shanty town. We all congregated at the shop opposite the baths, and the bus left us. Very quickly a huge and noisy crowd gathered.

We had to wait quite a while before Charlie could take the children to the baths. There were 9 of them and they were refused admission. Then we all went to the swimming pool and lined up behind the children, continually requesting permission to enter. Charlie started talking to the crowd, but there was a lot of hissing and booing. Then he went to the front of the line and when he refused to move was grabbed and taken away from the line. Then John Powell, Lou, Beth, Alex, myself and a couple of others were removed by the mayor first asking us if we would move, us saying no (individually) and then they put their hand on our backs and took us away from the line. Chris Page sat down and was carried off.

Those of us who had been walked off were prevented from rejoining the line as we had intended. Angry discussion broke out everywhere. I have never met such hostile, hate-filled people. The hostility seemed to be directed at us as university student intruders rather than to the aborigines …

CHARLES PERKINS, *A BASTARD LIKE ME*, 1975

And the crowd came, hundreds of them. They were pressing about twenty deep around the gate. Then the police arrived. They had received instructions by this time from the Labor Party which was in power in New South Wales at that time, to lay off us. 'Don't do anything that will cause any controversy with these people. Go with them as far as you can', seemed to be government advice to the police … the whole of the police force from Moree and surrounding towns were called in … the mayor of the town rolled up. (Recently when I went to Moree he shook my hand and reflected on what a good thing the Freedom Ride was for the town. But at that time it was a different story.)

LETTER, PHILIP HAYWARD TO ANN CURTHOYS, 1 JUNE 1994

With my wife and family I was resident in the Moree district for many years both before and after that date. My wife and I were both active in the Moree Aboriginal Advancement Society and in church, school, and public affairs … The churches, the schools and the Aboriginal Advancement Society had worked for a number of years to bring about the easing of tension. The Moree Municipal council controlled the town baths, from where aborigines were barred. But those who favoured the lifting of this ban had after many years achieved a majority on Council and were planning to have the ban lifted. Then along came the Freedom riders. Such was the antagonism they engendered in the town and among the aldermen that the aldermen decided that they would not move at that time, not wanting it to be thought that they were being 'railroaded' into a decision. So they deliberately withheld their move for a few months. So what was then seen as being a result of the 'Freedom Ride' was in fact a decision delayed for six months because of the 'Freedom Ride'.

While there is a common emotional resonance to these accounts, they are told from different perspectives, and many of the details are different. I am one of my own sources, writing a diary as a 19-year-old participant, and again as an intrepid historical researcher many years later. I like the effect of these juxtapositions, and the challenge they provide to the reader. Yet collage of this kind, made up of juxtaposed quotes from my various sources, will not in fact form the dominant mode of narration in the book. While it needs a form of narrative that draws attention to its specific grounding in time and place and to the impossibility of a unified narrative, it also needs a story that is accessible, compelling and strong. In searching for the appropriate narrative voice, I have played with various ways of representing different points of view, as well as with anti-chronological organisation, theoretical asides, and much else. I have pondered the idea of representing different voices in specific typefaces, as Richard Price did in *Alabi's World*.[2] I have played with Peter Burke's ideas of adopting some of the techniques of the modernist novel, such as the unreliable narrator or alternative endings.[3]

On a practical level, how can I refer to myself as an actor in an event that occurred in 1965? Should I say 'she' for the person I was, who no longer exists, or 'I'? (I've settled on 'I', as 'she' seems a little ridiculous.) Should the group of students of which I was one be referred to as 'they' or 'we'? 'They' seems unnaturally distant, a false objectivity perhaps, while 'we' is much too close, suggesting far too much unity between the historian and largely forgotten events of over thirty years ago. I'm working with 'they'. So far, the mixture of 'I' and 'they' is working out fine.

I have also had to confront the question of writing inter-racial history, a history of relations between indigenous and non-indigenous people in Australia, an ongoing history to which I belong on the non-indigenous side. There are ethical as well as stylistic problems, of finding a voice which is honest and true, which does not try to appropriate other people's stories, which embodies a full recognition that there is no objective space outside our racialised histories from which to write. In this context the reflexive 'I' becomes even more important.

In the end, I have adopted a reasonably straightforward narrative approach. My publisher has urged that I leave historiographical reflection to the end, and the marketing people have insisted that I keep a strong personal note, a strong authentic 'I' voice, if the book is to sell. The conventional aspects of the book include a rejection of self-consciously fictional elements, and sticking rigorously to my sources, whether these be written, oral or visual. I have settled also on a chronological structure; after the prologue I go back several decades, and move forward from there. I have only one typeface, and hope from the writing itself to do the job different typefaces achieve, that is to let the reader know about different voices, in some tension with one another.

On the other hand, the book does aspire to *some* postmodern elements. I have tried to foreground my own role as historian, former participant and writer. The chronological structure is disturbed by flashes back and forth in time. I have not seen it as possible to present a single explanation for the events I describe, preferring to present within my narrative a range of competing and possible understandings, each of which has validity if certain presuppositions are made. My own involvement, complicity perhaps, seems to make it all the more imperative that interpretation is left open, for others to disagree with or judge as they will.

And that is where it stands at the moment, with a whole lot written, and a book still in the process of emergence. Occasionally I panic that the project is so difficult, and my life so burdened with other responsibilities, that I will never get it done at all.[4]

ENDNOTES

[1] See P. Read's detailed account, *Charles Perkins: A Biography*, Viking, Ringwood, 1990.

[2] R. Price, *Alabi's World*, Johns Hopkins University Press, Baltimore, 1990.

[3] P. Burke, 'History of Events and the Revival of Narrative', in P. Burke (ed.), *New Perspectives on Historical Writing*, Polity Press, Cambridge, 1991, pp. 237–40. See my 'Sex and Racism: Australia in the 1960s', in Jane Long *et al.* (eds), *Forging Identities*, University of Western Australia Press, Nedlands, 1997, pp. 11–28.

[4] It was published as *Freedom Ride: A Freedomrider Remembers*, Allen & Unwin, Sydney, 2002.

CHAPTER 10

GALLERY, MUSEUM AND OTHER EXERCISES FOR WRITING HISTORY

Ann Curthoys
Ann McGrath

We used these writing exercises in our Visiting Scholars Program, and student response was very favourable. Try them in your writing class or informal writing group, or try them alone.

EXERCISE ONE: 'TWO WORDS'

When a group is first established, and first meets to discuss writing, arrange for everyone to introduce themselves, not only with some personal details and a statement of their subject or topic, but also by saying what their project is really about in two words. Just two words to suggest their major aim or purpose. Many people find this extraordinarily challenging, and thought-provoking.

A variant is to ask them to state the argument or theme of their project in one sentence.

EXERCISE TWO: KEEPING A DAILY JOURNAL

The daily journal is a great way to become more conscious of where you are going in the learning process. It serves as a sounding board for evolving ideas, and also as a means of mapping your achievement in developing a more sophisticated understanding of your research topic.

Write a daily journal entry that especially considers your writing project and ideas you encounter in primary research, secondary reading or seminar paper attendance which might have some bearing on your writing project. Feel free to write or illustrate (photos? doodles?) whatever else you like in it. This journal could then be used as a primary source for a reflective consideration of the research process.

We asked students to select an excerpt from their journal to read out to the class. Several chose to do a little editing for effect. The other students really enjoyed hearing the excerpts. The presentation stage should take place towards the end of the course or program—that is, once students have already gained a sense of trust, and a sense of having shared an intellectual journey.

EXERCISE THREE: WRITING OUT OF ART

Approximately 1000 words

This exercise aims to spark the imagination, especially of the visual and the metaphorical. For history writers, we see it as a 'warm up' exercise. You are encouraged to explore connections between visual creativity—the artist's practice/techniques of creating an image—and of the practice of creating academic writing. Technique (including the carefully learnt and the spontaneous) and audience response are important considerations.

The writer or teacher chooses an appropriate art exhibition which would be of interest. This exercise is designed as a class activity, but it can also be done by the individual writer, who might like to share the process with a writer colleague, or else to do this as an individual exercise. For our Writing Histories/Writing Cultures program, we took the students to an exhibition of Emily Kngwarreye's paintings at the National Gallery of Australia. When we took them to the 'Seeing Cézanne' exhibition at the Drill Hall Gallery, Australian National University, we asked Roger Benjamin, an art historian, to do a floor talk. Many galleries have educational officers and volunteers who will provide some introduction to an exhibition, but this is not essential.

We then asked students to write about 1000 words on either:

(a) Consider particular examples of art, or your overall visit to the Gallery, as a starting point. Write a reflexive, reflective piece about your training and experience as an academic writer, and muse about the borderlines between art and writing—craft, practice and effect upon audiences.

or

(b) Using one piece of art in particular, write an imaginative, richly descriptive piece based on your understandings of an aspect of an historical, possibly cross-cultural, experience or event/s. (You might consider writing dialogue and/or the first person, but at least experiment with some stylistic device you normally wouldn't use.)

We urged students to stretch their imaginations, to adopt an entirely new speaking voice and writing style. One of the gratifying aspects of this exercise was to see the students with flatter writing styles making long-distance creative leaps. Sometimes this led to a kind of identity crisis—'Was that me writing that?' All students circulated their work and the pieces were discussed one by one in the larger group. Discussion was lively and there was plenty of diversity in audience reactions to writing experimentation. While a consensus usually emerged about what 'had worked' and what hadn't, audience members will differ in taste and sensibility. Don't expect a homogenous audience!

EXERCISE FOUR

Approximately 1000 words

This is really a variant of Exercise Three but this time the focus is an object or objects in a museum.

Visit a specific museum exhibition—definitely not the whole museum—and write an imaginative narrative piece focussing upon an object or objects within the display. Experimentation with dialogue and rich scene-setting is encouraged.

You can do the same thing, with variations, with a play, film, or music.

EXERCISE FIVE

Approximately 3000 words, illustrated

This is a longer, more complex exercise, appropriate once a history-writing group is well established.

Select a building of heritage significance. Document it by observation and visual recording via photos, drawings, diagrams, maps. Using at least one primary source and historical background information, see if you can write a piece which brings the history of the building to life. Pay careful attention to the integration of visual and textual sections. (The responsible Heritage, Historic Houses or other organisation should have some background information to start off your research.)

EXERCISE SIX

Approximately 4000 words

Select a landscape or streetscape. This may be one you know well from personal experience or one which is a new area of inquiry. Describe what it looks like as richly as possible, then tell its story imaginatively. Pay careful attention to relations between people and the physical, tangible environment and draw diagrams and use photographs or other illustration where appropriate.

EXERCISE SEVEN

Approximately 5000 words

What is the topic of your main research project? Write a reflexive or reflective piece explaining how you came to choose it, or how it chose you. Now concentrate on describing the events of your research journey in as much detail as possible. Make sure it is a readable tale with strong introductory lead in, meaty discussion, and a clever ending.

CHAPTER 11

HOW TO WORKSHOP YOUR WRITING

Ann Curthoys
Ann McGrath

A writing workshop is an intensive small discussion group designed to provide an instant readership and supportive environment for improving your writing. The work in progress is distributed beforehand to all members of the group, or perhaps read out to the group (sometimes both), and then discussed. The group members respond to the piece of writing, saying what works, and making suggestions for improvement. Such workshops are common-place for fiction writers, especially in writing courses run by colleges, universities and other educational organisations. Writing groups are, in fact, everywhere.

Playwrights must workshop; it's integral to the craft of writing plays. Workshopping will make their play work, so they value it. They admit to the dangers of it causing crushed egos and over-indulgence in drink. Playwrights must have actors 'read' to check the sound and veracity of dialogue. Before a character can speak, they must stage-test to ensure they have inserted an instruction such as 'Enter stage' and have organised the entrances to avoid a collision with another actor entering simultaneously. The instruction 'Go through door' is only appropriate if the set designers are instructed to provide a door. Actors will refuse to say certain lines if they can't make sense of them. And that's all before the director comes on the scene to worry about the finer points of dramatic intensity, highs and lows, and the complex mix of music, sound effects, good casting and possibly consulting with the writer to alter the script.

In contrast, many people who write history have never really had their writing workshopped or openly discussed in a small group context. History writers will deliver a conference or a seminar paper, but that is more to get some useful feedback on its content rather than its style. In Australia, a conference or seminar paper in History is usually an oral delivery; rarely is a full written paper distributed. The audience may engage, they may come up with some stimulating new directions or useful critiques, but no one really mentions style. 'Wouldn't it be better to start in the middle and emphasise the first point and leave out that long quote?' 'Five minutes into the paper your expression was really vague.' Nobody would make such comments and, anyway, the spoken paper may differ completely from the longer chapter or other finished work. Many will also circulate their writing piece to their spouse and a colleague or two in a similar field—if there is such a person nearby—but, once again, feedback is more likely to be about content than style. Postgraduate students rely on their supervisor, usually a lone individual with a particular take on writing. Rather than wide audience satisfaction or appeal, the supervisor's priorities are what the examiners might think and whether the overall argument is coherent. History students and, for that matter, most other writers of history, write alone, then send off their product to a 'marker', journal editor or book publisher. The mechanics of writing — of structure and style — are thought to be either less important or already learnt somewhere else. Consequently there is no forum in which the writing itself can be beaten into shape.

All this is a great shame. Workshopping really works. Our own experience of workshopping with draft chapters of theses by postgraduate students was exhilarating. Workshopping can really improve your writing, provide a deadline, and be stimulating and enjoyable. Our students complained they wanted more of it — more sessions, longer sessions, more hours.

If you are not a teacher setting up a student group, we would recommend you take the drag-net approach, and invite any group of writing people you know to start a writing group. Any size will do, but we would suggest three as a minimum, and a maximum of eight. This might be a group of fellow students, fellow historians, or a mixed bunch of writers in various non-academic fields. Our workshop group included people from very diverse backgrounds and walks of life, as well as different academic disciplines. Although they were all postgraduates, participants included a retired policeman, a park ranger, an ex-filmmaker, an art historian and practising photographer, an architect who'd turned postmodernist poet, and the list went on. Admittedly there was a slightly disproportionate representation of projects on adventurous mountain-climbing women, but no two of the students were writing on the same subject. Everyone was able to train their minds to take some different directions and approaches, so they easily engaged in very disparate topics and writing styles. Our workshop participants had in common the writing of their postgraduate theses, but we were encouraging them to go against the grain. They were urged to break out, write creatively, and consider a wider, popular audience for their writing. Like many writers, they also shared the virtue of being good readers, and they read the other participants' work carefully indeed. More heads together means more ideas, and a truer sense of a real audience response.

We broke the group of twelve into two groups of six, and each was joined by at least one more senior person. But the workshops would have worked equally well if they were entirely student-run. The workshop could be chaired by anyone in the group and two longish papers can be discussed in a two to three hour meeting. You'd probably schedule a tea-break for the longer time slot. Participants read the papers in advance. Most of the papers were about 8000 words so they required an hour and a half each to discuss in detail. All kinds of issues were discussed.

You do need some ground rules. Our main rules were that it was important to say what we liked about a paper, and that any criticisms had to be constructive, in the form of suggestions for change. We used the format of going around the group in turn, so that each participant made comments. The whole group joined in to discuss them, to agree or disagree. 'I liked this bit.' 'This was funny.' 'This was clever.' 'That was moving.' Conversations about what was worthwhile were followed by the critique of aspects thought *not* to work so well, whether these be stylistic or conceptual. The writer was part of the workshop group and free to join in, stay quiet, or defend her or his work. Most were thrilled with the interest taken in their writing and very appreciative of input. Before the workshop phase, leaders might consider ways of encouraging students to work together in group discussions or get used to each other on an excursion or at a social gathering. Mutual trust is also engendered by the group leaders relating stories of their own writing experiences, or by reading out selections from their own work in progress or other recent work. Such sharing creates a mood for a mutually supportive atmosphere. But let's be honest, the first time your work is workshopped can be somewhat intimidating. On the other hand, it is an equitable arrangement, with all workshop members having turns at being critic and being critiqued. A helpful, respectful attitude ideally emerges, although there'd be the inevitable personality clash which might require mediating, or a dominating talker who might need to be told to queue for his or her next turn. One or two participants might get edgy and feel they have to justify their work at any cost. This is natural enough, for who hasn't felt insecure about their writing? Yet often the criticisms which surprise or upset us most are the useful ones. We only realise this with more distance. The reader is your audience, and if they don't clap much, you might as well know why. Most participants, however, will see the virtue of the suggestions they receive. Group members seem to really engage with and enjoy reading other writers' work and this gives them more confidence about self-editing and critique. Given their lack of experience in workshopping, the incisive and useful critiques and suggestions offered by postgraduates of their peers surprised us. Yet perhaps the high quality should be expected, for students have been trained to be good readers and critics, and have acquired many skills of their own making. The wonderful talent pool of potential peer-critics out there, with their strong conceptual skills, eyes for good writing and fresh ideas, are a wonderful resource that should not be wasted.

An audience, and an engaged, interactive audience of fellow readers and writers, can help you extend your own creativity. They can show you how to take a path that leads you further towards your chosen direction. They can show you how to make your work more effective, more memorable and inspiring.

It's great to learn from each other, and it provides a terrific ongoing support network from people who inevitably suffer similar kinds of writerly highs and lows. It extends the input, ideas and skills that will show in the final product. It will extend your range of lunch partners. Yes, the lonely writer gets to enjoy the company of fellow humans, plus gains an excellent excuse to phone that new friend. The recommended line is in plain language which cuts straight to the point: 'Want to start a writing workshop?'

CHAPTER 12

WRITING HISTORIES: A READING GUIDE AND BIBLIOGRAPHY

Kate McCarthy

THEORY, METAPHOR AND POETICS OF HISTORY-WRITING

The following works consider the theory of writing, or explore literary devices and strategies which are used in historical writing. This guide also lists some introductory guides to various 'difficult' theorists such as Foucault and de Certeau.

Abelove, H. *et al.* (eds), *Visions of History: Interviews with E.P. Thompson et al.*, Manchester University Press, Manchester, 1983.

Ankersmit, F.R., 'Historiography and Postmodernism', *History and Theory*, vol. 28, no. 2, 1989, pp. 137–53.

Ankersmit, F.R., *History and Tropology: The Rise and Fall of Metaphor*, University of California Press, Los Angeles, 1994.

Ankersmit, F.R. and Kellner, H. (eds), *A New Philosophy of History*, Reaktion Books, London, 1995.

Arac, J. (ed.), *After Foucault: Humanistic Knowledge, Postmodern Challenges*, Rutgers University Press, New Brunswick, 1988.

Arendt, H., 'Introduction', in W. Benjamin, *Illuminations* (1955), Schocken Books, New York, 1985, pp. 38–51.

Ashplant, T.G., 'Fantasy, Narrative, Event: Psychoanalysis and History', *History Workshop Journal*, no. 23, 1987, pp. 165–73.

Barthes, R., 'Historical Discourse', in M. Lane (ed.), *Introduction to Structuralism*, Basic Books, New York, 1970, pp. 145–55.

Barthes, R., 'The Death of the Author', in *Image, Music, Text*, essays selected and trans. by S. Heath, Hill and Wang, New York, 1977, pp. 142–48.

Berkhofer, R.F., *Beyond the Great Story: History as Text and Discourse*, The Belknap Press of Harvard University Press, Cambridge, Mass., 1995.

Bloch, M., *The Historian's Craft*, trans. P. Putnam, Manchester University Press, Manchester, 1967.

Braudel, F., *On History*, Weidenfield and Nicolson, London, 1980.

Brennan, T., 'The Public Face of the "Third World" Writer', in his *At Home in the World: Cosmopolitanism Now*, Harvard University Press, Cambridge, Mass., 1997, pp. 36–44.

Burke, P., (ed.), *New Perspectives on Historical Writing*, Polity Press, Cambridge, 1991.

Chartier, R., *Cultural History*, Polity Press, Cambridge, 1988.

Clendinnen, I., 'Fellow Sufferers: History and Imagination', *Australian Humanities Review*, 1997–98, electronic journal at http://www.australianhumanitiesreview.org/.

Clendinnen, I., *The History Question: Who Owns the Past?*, Black Inc, Melbourne, 2006.

Clendinnen, I., *Reading the Holocaust*, Text, Melbourne, 1998.

Clendinnen, I., *True Stories* (The 1999 Boyer Lectures), ABC Books, Sydney, 1999.

Clifford J. and Marcus, G., *Writing Culture: The Poetics and Politics of Ethnography*, University of California Press, Berkeley, 1986.

Curthoys, A. and Docker, J., *Is History Fiction?*, University of New South Wales Press, Sydney, and Michigan University Press, Ann Arbor, 2005.

Curthoys, A. and Docker, J., 'Is History Fiction?', *UTS Review*, vol. 2, no. 1, 1996, pp. 12–37.

Curthoys, A. and Docker, J., 'The Two Histories', *Rethinking History*, vol. 1, no. 3, 1997, pp. 259–73.

Curthoys, A., and Docker, J., 'Time, Eternity, Truth, and Death: History as Allegory', *Humanities Research*, no. 1, 1999, pp. 5–26.

de Certeau, M., *The Certeau Reader*, edited by G. Ward, Blackwell, Oxford, 2000.

de Certeau, M., *Heterologies: Discourse on the Other*, University of Minnesota Press, Minneapolis, 1986.

de Certeau, M., *The Writing of History*, Columbia University Press, New York, 1988.

Dening, G., *Mr Bligh's Bad Language: Passion, Power, and Theatre on the Bounty*, Cambridge University Press, Cambridge, 1992.

Dening, G., 'A Poetic for Histories', in his *Performances*, Melbourne University Press, Melbourne, 1996, pp. 35–63.

Dening, G., 'The Theatricality of History Making and the Paradoxes of Acting', *Cultural Anthropology*, vol. 8, no. 1, 1993, pp. 73–95.

Dening, G., 'Writing, Rewriting the Beach', *Rethinking History*, vol. 2, no. 2, 1998, pp. 143–72.

Derrida, J., *Of Grammatology*, Johns Hopkins University Press, Baltimore, 1980.

Derrida, J., 'White Mythology: Metaphor in the Text of Philosophy', in J. Derrida, *Margins of Philosophy*, trans. Alan Bass, University of Chicago Press, Chicago, 1982, pp. 207–71.

Derrida, J., *Writing and Difference*, University of Chicago Press, Chicago, 1978.

Easthope, A., 'Romancing the Stone: History-Writing and Rhetoric', *Social History*, vol. 18, no. 2, 1993, pp. 235–49.

Fabian, J., *Time and the Other: How Anthropology Makes its Object*, Columbia University Press, New York, 1983.

Foucault, M., *The Archaeology of Knowledge*, trans. A.M. Sheridan Smith, Tavistock Publications, London, 1972.

Foucault, M., *Discipline and Punish: The Birth of the Prison*, trans. A. Sheridan, Allen Lane, London, 1977.

Foucault, M., *The History of Sexuality: An Introduction*, trans. R. Hurley, Vintage Books, New York, 1980.

Foucault, M., 'Nietzsche, Genealogy, History', in D.F. Bouchard (ed.), *Language, Counter-Memory, Practice: Selected Essays and Interviews*, Cornell University Press, Ithaca, 1977, pp. 139–64.

Foucault, M., *The Order of Things: An Archaeology of the Human Sciences*, Tavistock Publications, London, 1970.

Foucault, M., 'Truth and Power', interview published in C. Gordon (ed.), *Power/Knowledge: Selected Interviews and Other Writings, 1972–1977*, Pantheon Books, New York, 1980, pp. 109–33.

Foucault, M., 'What is an Author?', in D.F. Bouchard (ed.), *Language, Counter-Memory, Practice: Selected Essays and Interviews by Michel Foucault*, Cornell University Press, Ithaca, 1977, pp. 113–38.

Frow, J., *Time and Commodity Culture: Essays in Cultural Theory and Postmodernity*, Clarendon Press, Oxford, 1997.

Gay, P., *Style in History*, Basic Books, New York, 1974.

Geertz, C., 'History and Anthropology', *New Literary History*, vol. 21, no. 2, 1990, pp. 321–35.

Geertz, C., 'Thick Description: Toward an Interpretive Theory of Culture', in his *The Interpretation of Cultures*, Basic Books, New York, 1973, pp. 3–30.

Gossman, L., 'History and Literature: Reproduction or Signification', in R.H. Canary and H. Kozicki (eds), *The Writing of History: Literary Form and Historical Understanding*, University of Wisconsin Press, Madison, 1978, pp. 233–48.

Grenville, K., *Searching for the Secret River*, Text Publishing, Melbourne, 2006.

Grenville, K., 'History and Fiction', in *Australian Quarterly Essay*, no. 25, also available at http://www.users.bigpond.com/kgrenville/TSR/history_and_fiction.html.

Gross, E., 'Philosophy, Subjectivity and the Body: Kristeva and Irigaray', in C. Pateman and E. Gross (eds), *Feminist Challenges: Social and Political Theory*, Allen & Unwin, Sydney, 1986, pp. 125–43.

Halttunen, K., 'Cultural History and the Challenge of Narrativity', in V.E. Bonnell and L. Hunt (eds), *Beyond the Cultural Turn: New Directions in the Study of Society and Culture*, University of California Press, Berkeley, 1998, pp. 165–81.

Harvey, D., 'Postmodernism', in his *The Condition of Postmodernity: An Enquiry into the Origins of Cultural Change*, Johns Hopkins University Press, Baltimore, 1989, pp. 39–65.

Hoy, D.C. (ed.), *Foucault: A Critical Reader*, Basil Blackwell, Oxford, 1986.

Hunt, L. (ed.), *The New Cultural History*, University of California Press, Berkeley, 1989.

Hutcheon, L., *A Poetics of Postmodernism: History, Theory, Fiction*, Routledge, New York, 1988.

Jay, P., *Being in the Text: Self-Representation from Wordsworth to Roland Barthes*, Cornell University Press, Ithaca, 1984.

Jenkins, K., *On 'What is History?': From Carr and Elton to Rorty and White*, Routledge, London, 1995.

Jenkins, K., *Re-Thinking History*, Routledge, London, 1991.

Jenkins, K. (ed.), *The Postmodern History Reader*, Routledge, London, 1997.

La Capra, D., *Rethinking Intellectual History: Texts, Contexts, Language*, Cornell University Press, Ithaca, 1983.

La Capra, D., *Soundings in Critical Theory*, Cornell University Press, Ithaca, 1988.

Limerick, P., 'Making the Most of Words: Verbal Activity and Western America', in W. Cronon *et al.* (eds), *Under an Open Sky: Rethinking America's Western Past*, W.W. Norton, New York, 1992, pp. 167–84.

Lloyd, G., *Being in Time: Selves and Narrators in Philosophy and Literature*, Routledge, London, 1993.

Lyotard, J., *The Postmodern Condition: A Report on Knowledge*, trans. G. Bennington and B. Massumi, University of Minnesota Press, Minneapolis, 1984.

McGrath, A., 'The Female Eunuch in the Suburbs: Reflections on Adolescence, Autobiography and History-Writing', *Journal of Popular Culture*, vol. 33, no. 1, 1999, pp. 177–90.

McKenna, M., 'Writing the Past', in Drusilla Modjeska (ed.), *Best Australian Essays 2006*, Black Inc, Melbourne, 2006, pp. 96–110.

Merwick, D., 'Postmodernism and the Possibilities of Representation', *Australasian Journal of American Studies*, vol. 10, no. 1, 1991, pp. 1–10.

Nietzsche, F.W., *Untimely Meditations*, trans R.J. Hollingdale, Cambridge University Press, New York, 1983.

Philipp, J., 'Traditional Historical Narrative and Action Oriented (or Ethnographic) History', *Historical Studies*, vol. 20, no. 80, 1983, pp. 339–52.

Reekie, G., 'Michel de Certeau and the Poststructuralist Critique of History', *Social Semiotics*, vol. 6, no. 1, 1996, pp. 45–49.

Ricoeur, P., *Time and Narrative*, vol. 1, trans. K. McLaughlin and D. Pellauer, University of Chicago Press, Chicago, 1984.

Rigney, A., *The Rhetoric of Historical Representation: Three Narrative Histories of the French Revolution*, Cambridge University Press, Cambridge, 1990.

Said, E.W., *Beginnings: Intention and Method*, Johns Hopkins University Press, Baltimore, 1975.

Said, E.W., *Orientalism*, Random House, New York, 1978.

Said, E.W., *The World, the Text, and the Critic*, Faber and Faber, London, 1984.

Siebenschuh, W.R., *Fictional Techniques and Factual Works*, University of Georgia Press, Athens, Georgia, 1983.

Somekawa, E. and Smith E., 'Theorizing the Writing of History or "I Can't Think Why It Should Be So Dull, For a Great Deal Of It Must Be Invention"', *Journal of Social History*, vol. 22, no. 1, 1988, pp. 149–61.

Spivak, G., 'Subaltern Studies: Deconstructing Historiography', in Ranajit Guha (ed.), *Subaltern Studies, IV: Writings on South Asian History*, Oxford University Press, Delhi, 1985, pp. 330–63.

Stock, B., 'Literary Discourse and the Social Historian', in his *Listening for the Text: On the Uses of the Past*, Johns Hopkins University Press, Baltimore, 1990, pp. 75–94.

White, H., 'The Burden of History', *History and Theory*, vol. 5, no. 2, 1966, pp. 111–34.

White, H., *The Content of the Form: Narrative Discourse and Historical Representation*, Johns Hopkins University Press, Baltimore, 1987.

White, H., *Metahistory: The Historical Imagination in Nineteenth Century Europe*, Johns Hopkins University Press, Baltimore, 1973.

White, H., 'The Value of Narrativity in the Representation of Reality', *Critical Inquiry*, vol. 7, no. 4, 1981, pp. 5–27.

Windschuttle, K., *The Killing of History: How a Discipline is Being Murdered by Literary Critics and Social Theorists*, Macleay Press, Sydney, 1994.

Young, R., *White Mythologies: Writing History and the West*, Routledge, London, 1990.

For theoretical considerations when writing history, see also a number of journals including: *History and Theory, Rethinking History*, and *History Workshop Journal*.

DEBATES OVER HISTORY

Macintyre, S., with Clark, A., *The History Wars*, Melbourne University Publishing, Melbourne, 2003.

Attwood, B., *Telling the Truth about Aboriginal History*, Allen & Unwin, Sydney, 2005.

WRITING GUIDES

Anderson, J. and Poole, M., *Thesis and Assignment Writing*, 2nd edition, John Wiley and Sons, Brisbane, 1994.

Bates, D., *The New Writer's Survival Guide: An Introduction to the Craft of Writing*, Penguin, Ringwood, 1989.

Cameron, J., *The Right To Write: An Invitation and Initiation to the Writing Life*, Macmillan, London, 2000.

Dillard, A., *The Writing Life*, Pan Books, London, 1990.

Dunn, I., *The Writer's Guide: A Companion to Writing for Pleasure or Publication*, Allen & Unwin, Sydney, 1999.

Evans, D.G., *How to Write a Better Thesis or Report*, Melbourne University Press, Melbourne, 1995.

Germano, W., *Getting it Published: A Guide for Scholars and Anyone Else Serious about Serious Books*, University of Chicago Press, Chicago, 2001.

Grenville, K., *The Writing Book: A Workbook for Fiction Writers*, Allen & Unwin, Sydney, 1990.

Harman, E. *et al.*, *The Thesis and the Book: A Guide for First-Time Academic Authors*, 2nd edn, University of Toronto Press, Toronto, 2003.

Orwell, G., 'Politics and the English Language', in *The Collected Essays, Journalism and Letters*, vol. 4, Penguin, London, 1970, pp. 156–70.

Oxford Australian Writers' Dictionary, S. Purchase (ed.), Oxford University Press, Melbourne, 1997.

Preece, R.A., *Starting Research: An Introduction to Academic Research and Dissertation Writing*, Printer Publishers, London, 1994.

Miller, P., *Writing Your Life: A Journey of Discovery*, Allen & Unwin, Sydney, 1994.

Murray-Smith, S., *Right Words: A Guide to English Usage in Australia*, Penguin, Ringwood, 2nd edition, 1990.

Strunk, W. and White, E.B., *The Elements of Style*, Macmillan, New York, 1979.

Tredinnick, M., *The Little Green Grammar Book*, University of New South Wales Press, Sydney, 2008.

Tredinnick, M., *The Little Red Writing Book*, University of New South Wales Press, Sydney, 2006.

Watson, G., *Writing a Thesis: A Guide to Long Essays and Dissertations* (1987), Longman, London, 1996.

EXAMPLES OF GOOD WRITING—HISTORICAL AND OTHERWISE

The following include some disparate examples of writing that are valuable in a number of ways. They offer a guide to the various styles and methodologies which can characterise historical writing, as well as presenting examples of clear, precise and powerful writing. Included are works cited by the various historians who participated in the Visiting Scholars Program as examples of good historical writing, and books they wished they had written.

Agnew, J., *Worlds Apart: The Market and the Theater in Anglo-American Thought 1550–1750*, Cambridge University Press, Cambridge, 1988.

Clark, C.M.H., *The Puzzles of Childhood*, Viking, Ringwood, 1989.

Clark, C.M.H., *The Quest for Grace*, Viking, Ringwood, 1990.

Clenndinnen, I., 'Agamemnon's Kiss', in P. Craven (ed.), *The Best Australian Essays 1998*, Bookman Press, Melbourne, 1998, pp. 206–16.

Clenndinnen, I., *Dancing with Strangers*, Text, Melbourne, 2003.

Cochrane, P., *Colonial Ambition: Foundations of Australian Democracy*, Melbourne University Publishing, Melbourne, 2006.

Darian-Smith, K. and Hamilton, P. (eds), *Memory and History in Twentieth Century Australia*, Oxford University Press, Melbourne, 1994.

Darnton, R., 'Workers Revolt: The Great Cat Massacre of the Rue Saint-Severin', in his *The Great Cat Massacre and Other Episodes in French Cultural History*, Allen Lane, London, 1984, pp. 75–104.

Fussell, P., 'Theater of War', in his *The Great War and Modern Memory*, Oxford University Press, Oxford, 1975, pp. 191–230.

Haraway, D., 'Situated Knowledges: The Science Question in Feminism and the Privilege of Partial Perspective', *Feminist Studies*, vol. 14, no. 3, 1988, pp. 575–99.

Michaels, A., *Fugitive Pieces*, Bloomsbury, London, 1997.

Modjeska, D., *Stravinsky's Lunch*, Picador, Sydney, 1999.

Orwell, G., 'Shooting an Elephant', in his *Inside the Whale and Other Essays*, Penguin, Harmondsworth, 1962, pp. 91–99.

Price, R., *Alabi's World*, Johns Hopkins University Press, Baltimore, 1990.

Price, R., *The Convict and the Colonel*, Beacon Press, Boston, 1998.

Schama, S., *Landscape and Memory*, HarperCollins Publishers, London, 1995.

Thompson, E.P., *The Making of the English Working Class* (1963), Penguin, Harmondsworth, 1980.

Thompson, E.P., 'Time, Work-Discipline and Industrial Capitalism', *Past and Present*, no. 38, 1967, pp. 56–97.

Watson, D., *Caledonia Australis: Scottish Highlanders on the Frontier of Australia*, Collins, Sydney, 1984.

CONTRIBUTORS

At the time this book was first published all the contributors were based at The Australian National University. Now, their respective affiliations are:

Ann Curthoys, Department of History, University of Sydney

John Docker, Department of History, University of Sydney, and Research School of Humanities, The Australian National University

Bill Gammage, Humanities Research Centre, The Australian National University

Tom Griffiths, History Program, Research School of Social Sciences, The Australian National University

Kate McCarthy, School of Law, University of Exeter

Ann McGrath, History Program, Research School of Social Sciences, The Australian National University

Donna Merwick, Centre for Cross-Cultural Research, The Australian National University

Peter Read, Department of History, University of Sydney

Deborah Bird Rose, Centre for Research on Social Inclusion, Macquarie University

At the time of his death in 2008, Greg Dening was Emeritus Professor of History at the University of Melbourne and Adjunct Professor at the Centre for Cross-Cultural Research, The Australian National University.